HAUNTED LITTLE ROCK

LINDA L. HOWELL

Haunted America

Published by Haunted America
A Division of The History Press
Charleston, SC 29403
www.historypress.net

First published 2012

Manufactured in the United States

ISBN 978.1.60949.407.0

Library of Congress Cataloging-in-Publication Data

Howell, Linda L.
Haunted Lttle Rock / Linda L. Howell.
p. cm.
ISBN 978-1-60949-407-0
1. Haunted places--Arkansas--Little Rock. 2. Ghosts--Arkansas--Little Rock. I. Title.
BF1472.U6H68 2012
133.109767'73--dc23
2012033005

Notice: The information in this book is true and complete to the best of our knowledge. It is offered without guarantee on the part of the author or The History Press. The author and The History Press disclaim all liability in connection with the use of this book.

CONTENTS

Acknowledgements

Those who are inspired to express their creative thoughts usually have backing from others. This book came about from someone asking me to write about the haunted places in the Little Rock area. It excites me when telling others about ghosts who haunt the homes and buildings in our city, but it's the experience that one has with the supernatural that makes you a true believer.

For centuries, my family has believed that an afterlife exists and a thin line or veil is what separates the human world from the spirit world. We are saddened when we lose a loved one, but if we accept the fact that they are in a beautiful place, perhaps that thought makes the grieving process less painful.

Communicating with the deceased is another matter and is quite possible with modern-day equipment. This undertaking should be done with caution because it is possible to contact some spirits that you'd rather not be in the company of, so tread softly.

I have many people in my life who have been instrumental in encouraging me to do haunted tours and write about the haunted places I'm familiar with. I would like to thank those who have supported me, for without them I would not have been able to complete this task.

And I would especially like to thank:

- First and foremost, my sister Alyson Hoge, who edited this book and earned the nickname "Iron Lady." I could not have done this without her.

- My brother-in-law, David Hoge, who patiently took the photographs for this book.
- My mother, Jeanne Bradley LaGrossa, who made my life interesting and encouraged my inquiring mind to search for information.
- My late father, James LaGrossa, who laughed at me when I said I wanted to contact him after his death. Although I haven't contacted him personally, he is in touch with one of my grandsons.
- My husband, Richard Howell, who accepts me as I am.
- My children, Patrick Howell and Kristine DeBrine and her husband, Robbie, who truly have inspired me to take on challenging tasks.
- My sister Camille LaGrossa, who once said, "You should write a book," which I did, about her farm.
- My grandsons, Tyler and Tayler DeBrine, who love my bedtime ghost stories. My granddaughter Sophie Grace Howell and her mother, Stephanie Howell, who like to visit my haunted sites.
- Gerri Wright, my friend of many years who has been supportive of me through thick and thin.
- Rhonda Burton, my good friend who opened the door for the spirit Mary Walters to come through and enter my life.
- Julia Burnelle "Bernie" Smade Babcock, truly my great-great-aunt, who believed in the afterlife and communicating with those on the other side…a unique individual.
- And last of all, Will McKay at The History Press, who sent me an e-mail one day asking me to write a book. Without him, this book would not exist.

INTRODUCTION

Reading this book will take you on a journey into the haunted history of Little Rock, Arkansas.

When I was presented with the opportunity to write about the haunted history of Little Rock, I gave great thought and consideration to the idea but asked myself, "Where do I start?"

So, I went to the place where it all began, *La Petite Roche*—the natural rock formation on the bank of the Arkansas River known as the "little rock."

As I parked my car and began walking toward it, the gentle breeze blowing across my face and the sound of the river lapping against the shoreline created a peaceful setting. It had been a long time since I had visited this location, and it had changed over the years. What used to be a rustic rocky riverbank was now a beautifully landscaped area—very pedestrian friendly. I came to the edge and looked down. There it was, the foothills of the Ouachita Mountains. Yes, this rock formation is part of that mountain chain—a fact that's hard to believe, but true.

As I looked around the area, I thought about the man who had discovered the rock and how much had changed since he first saw it. Years after his discovery, a railroad bridge was built on top of it and the footing established securely into its bed. Today, the bridge is a reconditioned pedestrian walkway used by people to travel back and forth across the river from Little Rock to North Little Rock.

I mentally took myself back into time and tried to envision the French explorers anchoring their boats to check out the site. It was in the mid-1700s

A postcard view of the outcropping of rock on the Arkansas River that French explorer Jean-Baptiste Bénard de La Harpe called *La Petit Roche.* The "little rock" for which the city is named is located in downtown Little Rock. *Postcard courtesy of the Karcher Candy Company.*

when French explorer Jean-Baptiste Bénard de La Harpe led a group of twenty-five men up the Arkansas River from where it joined the Mississippi. France wanted to develop trade routes in the south and west, and La Harpe was the best person to do this because he had made profitable discoveries from his other explorations.

La Harpe's journey began in 1722, when his entourage stopped at Arkansas Post, a settlement located at the confluence of the two rivers, and picked up supplies for their upstream journey. As he approached this area, the terrain changed and the group saw the first outcropping of rock on the bank of the river. Continuing upstream, they would see a large rocky bluff rising more than one hundred feet in the air.

As described in *The Encyclopedia of Arkansas History and Culture*, "ascending about 160 feet high (fifty meters) and veined with a very hard, marble-like stone; La Harpe also described a large waterfall and several fine slate quarries nearby. According to his journal, he named this point "Le Rocher Français" ('French Rock') and took possession of it on April 9 by carving the coat of arms of the French king on a tree trunk on its summit."

This location is where rock was excavated over the years and used in many different structures throughout the cities of Little Rock and North Little Rock. In fact, one of the chapters in this book is about the Tower Building in

MacArthur Park, and rock from this quarry was transported to Little Rock to be used in the foundation and base support of the building.

La Harpe had to give up on his plans to reach the headwaters of the Arkansas. The explorers lacked the supplies needed to finish the long journey. He traveled another seventy miles above Little Rock and discovered a large Quapaw Indian village before turning back. He kept a journal and wrote about his adventures in the New World. Some people, including historians, considered his stories somewhat "enhanced," but they were very important in this regard. His accounts were about the early exploration of land that would one day become part of the Louisiana Purchase.

Locally, we pay tribute to this man who some believe is responsible for the name of our city. One of our downtown streets is La Harpe Boulevard, which runs parallel with the river. According to *The Encyclopedia of Arkansas History and Culture*, La Harpe kept a journal and noted that the purpose of his trip was to search for "an Emerald Rock, a fabulous jewel-encrusted stone." An area in North Little Rock is called Emerald Park in honor of him. It's located on the summit of the big rock formation where he allegedly carved the French king's coat of arms into a tree trunk.

The *Arkansas Gazette* first described the "little rock" on August 20, 1822: "It projects several feet into the river, forming below it a fine basin for boats, and its top reaches perhaps about midway between the low-water mark and the summit of the bank of the river. The name *Little Rock* was given it by the aborigines, or the early white settlers of the country to distinguish it from the Big Rock."

After Arkansas became a territory, people began moving here from the eastern part of the United States. It was a long journey, but traveling by boat seemed the fastest way. The "little rock" served as a ferry landing, and as our city grew, more riverboats were docking along the river's edge down from the "rock." The river was the lifeblood of our town and has remained an important landmark.

The early settlers were professional people such as doctors, lawyers and businessmen. All wanted change, and coming to the new frontier territory seemed an ideal solution. Some of these early men and women are the spirits that haunt Little Rock today. They occupy their former homes, businesses, churches and just about any place that once meant something to them. Of course, the modern-day spirits are active also, and some occupy the same place together with their ghostly ancestors. Imagine what they must be talking about—if they do talk, that is.

Haunt, haunted, haunting: these words are defined by Webster as "to inhabit, visit, or appear to in the form of a ghost or other supernatural being." Webster also explains that a ghost is "the spirit of a dead person, especially one believed to appear in bodily likeness to living persons or to haunt former habitats." So if Webster has a definition for haunting and ghost, then they must exist. They are, after all, words in the dictionary.

Alas, not everyone who reads this will agree so. Certain religions believe in the Holy Spirit or Holy Ghost but don't necessarily accept the belief of a humanly spirit and consider it to be sacrilegious. I am not here to change anyone's beliefs or explain why I do accept the paranormal as very real.

Just to know that a form of life does exist after we die fascinates me and is what drives me to search for answers. If you approach this subject with an open mind, you'll be surprised to learn that everyone has experienced the supernatural. Ever wonder what touched your skin with a feathery stroke or where a passing fragrance came from that smelled of lavender, roses or a form of tobacco?

My daughter once smelled cigarette smoke in our home and questioned how it could happen since no one in the family smoked. I confessed that I too had experienced such an odor for the past several years but didn't mention it for fear of scaring other family members. I was right; it did scare her! My reluctance in admitting such an experience left me wondering how my family would have accepted it had I mentioned it earlier.

One of my favorite stories is about my sister's personal encounter. We were standing at the bedside of a family member who had just crossed over from life into death. My sister remarked about seeing, in her peripheral vision, a figure standing next to her. But when she turned to see who it was, there was no one there. This happened several times within an hour. My sister is a skeptic of the highest degree but knew she was having an unusual experience.

A movement or image in one's peripheral vision that is obvious enough to make you turn and check it out is a common occurrence and could be related to the paranormal. These are forms of contact from the spirit world, and they are universal.

Those who have seen an apparition describe it as mesmerizing. Imagine you're getting ready for bed, and as you turn off the lights, only a dim light radiates from the outside street into the room. As you begin your ascent to the upper floor, there you see a ghostly figure motioning for you to follow. Would you do so?

If you notice that things around you at home or work seem to be misplaced or put in another location, do you stop and think it might be a spirit trying to get your attention? I've known several people who have experienced these things.

A paranormal friend of mine mentioned that the office personnel where he worked began to notice that small things were disappearing from their desks overnight. It seemed that these objects would somehow leave one office and appear in a vacant office. How can this happen? It's just one of those unexplained events that suggest something other than a human has been causing it. The following story is about an experience that a friend of mine had in Little Rock. After you have read it, think about what you would have done in her situation.

I had prepared breakfast, cleaned up and fixed a school lunch for my son. He had just caught the bus and was on his way to school—my husband was at work. I wanted to crawl back in bed for more rest and to read a book. Just then, I heard footsteps in the kitchen and was able to look in that direction from my bed because of the location of the kitchen to my bedroom.

A man came from the kitchen, down a short hallway and into my bedroom. He was wearing a plaid shirt with khaki pants and work boots. He was in his forties and with dark hair. He approached me while I was in bed and sat on the edge looking into my eyes. No words were spoken, but he leaned his head and shoulders "into" my head and upper torso, sharing the same space as my body.

This time of "shared space" was brief, and he withdrew to look into my eyes again, as if to say, "I mean you no harm." He then leaned back into my physical space. I could sense that he wanted me to know that his death was not an accident. During the experience, I could feel a very small electric current sensation running throughout my body. It was as though I could feel my molecules vibrating. I was not afraid during this experience.

He left, and the vibration or current continued inside my body. I wanted to try and find out who he was and how he died. Thinking he may have come from my hometown and was reaching out to me, I contacted an old friend. I asked him to research the town paper and local resources to see if someone matching his description had died in a questionable way.

My friend came back with no results pertaining to my hometown. I thought perhaps the man had lived in my house, but I never followed through with checking into the house's history. I did know that it was built in 1909. It was located in an affluent neighborhood in Little Rock—the Heights.

While all this is going on, two weeks have passed and I'm still experiencing the electrical charge sensation. Due to this vibration, I experienced sleep disturbance and a growing discomfort with his "presence." Then I spoke

> *with a professional social worker friend. I decided to talk to the deceased man because I felt he was still with me and that was the electric sensation I was feeling. I felt as though it was almost a way that he could either monitor my actions, or maybe experience human actions/emotions, yet he didn't seem to want to dominate or influence.*
>
> *One day I positioned myself in the bedroom and started talking with hopes that he could hear and understand what I was about to say. I stated that I had done all I could do to find out who he was and what happened to cause his death. I told him that I was not fearful, nor meant him any harm, but suggested that he must separate from me both physically and spiritually.*
>
> *I said that I witnessed his distress at his death not being an accident, but suggested he must move on. I was his witness. I acknowledged his untimely passing and honored his life. At that time, the tingling sensation left my body, and I have never felt it again. I also did not see him during this experience. He did not remain in the house.*

Now it is time to read the pages before you. Each chapter was written with a true knowledge and feeling of the spirits that occupy the structures. I never question why but accept that they do exist and have chosen to stay. There has never been an experience that I felt uncomfortable with, and I feel that these spirits are desperate to let us know they are OK. I hope that you come away with an appreciation of the "other side," for one day, we will be there too.

CHAPTER 1

THE HAUNTING OF CURRAN HALL

On July 4, 1843, Colonel Ebenezer Walters and his young wife, Mary Eliza, visited the construction site of their future home. It had been nearly a year since the work began, and the couple was anxious to move in and get settled before the birth of their first child. It was a very hot, steamy day, as was typical for Little Rock in July, but the Walterses disregarded that fact because they wanted to see their house.

They left after walking the property and were very happy with the progress. It would be finished in a few months, just in time for the birth of their baby. During the carriage ride back home, Mary was beginning to feel very weak. They were living with Chester Ashley, Mary's uncle, and upon arriving at his house, she went to bed.

The colonel thought his wife was suffering from the hot humid weather—he did not recognize that she was about to go into premature labor. It would be a long night, but he stayed by her bedside the entire time. She continued to get weaker, and for the next several days, her condition grew worse. No longer able to continue holding on, Mary and the baby died, leaving the colonel devastated. No one would have suspected at that time that Mary would one day haunt what would have been her home.

She and the baby were placed together in the same coffin and taken to Mount Holly Cemetery for burial. Located on the outskirts of town, the land had just been donated to the city by her uncle a few months earlier. She and her baby would be among the first burials in the new public cemetery.

There was sadness throughout the small community, and the colonel was so distraught that he felt the need to move far away from Little Rock. He was a member of the local militia and decided to join the forces in Texas and fight in the war against Mexico.

He asked the bank to sell the house, which it did to a local attorney. David Baldwin was a newlywed man and happy to bring his young bride to the Walterses' house. As sad as it was, the Baldwins were very happy and lived there for several years until a job change took them out of state.

The lengthy battle took its toll on Colonel Walters, and he suffered from the wounds he received in the war. Upon returning to Little Rock, he sought the comfort and care of family and friends. Although back home, he never returned to see his house. Death came knocking at the door on August 14, 1849, almost six years to the date of Mary's death. He was buried at Mount Holly Cemetery, beside his beloved wife and child.

The Walterses' house is known today as Curran Hall—so named for the second family who bought it from the Baldwins. Most of the owners were distinguished citizens of Little Rock and are part of our state's history.

During the mid-1800s, Arkansas was a bustling river port and heavily involved in the riverboat traffic. The city became a popular business and pleasure stop for those making their way up and down the Arkansas River. Little Rock was the state capital, and people were enthusiastic about the town's new growth. The small town had a reputation of being a nice place to live and settle down; that feeling is the same today.

The new citizens were busy constructing homes and buildings. Everything being built faced the river, and Curran Hall was no exception. Situated on a hillside several blocks from the river's edge, this house had a glorious view.

Since the Walterses and Baldwins were members of Little Rock's society, the house and surrounding grounds were in keeping with their status in the community. It was a small estate with a main house, detached kitchen, gardens and livestock, which were housed in the barn.

In 1849, another attorney, named James Moore Curran, and his wife, Sophie Fulton, bought the house and were looking forward to spending their lives together while raising their family. Sophie was the daughter of Arkansas' last territorial governor, William Savin Fulton.

They lived in the house for several years, raising their two children and enjoying the good life—and unaware that their lives were about to change.

The Little Rock Visitor Center is located in the restored antebellum home known as Curran Hall. It was built in 1843 by Colonel Ebenezer Walters for his young wife, Mary Eliza Walters. *Photo by David Hoge.*

Mr. Curran traveled extensively throughout the state providing legal counsel to his clients. He was a prosperous pioneer attorney, and his wealth was increasing as he accepted payment of land for services rendered.

After returning from one of his road trips, he became very sick, and although all attempts were made to nurse him back to health, he succumbed to pneumonia and died on October 6, 1854. His death was the first to take place in the house, and his young family was overwhelmed with grief.

Sophie was pregnant with their third child and gave birth to a daughter about four months later. She eventually married Curran's law partner, George Watkins, who was a widower with children of his own. They lived with their combined families at Curran Hall for several years, and Mr. Watkins became a chief justice of the Arkansas Supreme Court during that time.

The children from this union all became some of Little Rock's most prominent citizens and held positions as attorneys and doctors. The Curran daughters married into the "Dynasty," a name given to a group of people who were members of one of the four Arkansas politically powerful families. Known to dominate politics from statehood to the Civil War, they intermarried in order to maintain political control.

The Curran's youngest daughter, Alice Curran Conway, inherited the house but never lived in it with her family. She sold it to Jacob Herrmann Frolich and his wife, who resided there while he served as Arkansas' secretary of state. It was rumored that he created several trapdoors in the floor leading to secret chambers under the house.

Some of the townspeople seriously believed that Mr. Frolich was practicing magic at the house. This legend was probably based on Mr. Frolich's relative, Dr. Samuel Herrmann, known to be a famous magician called "Herrmann the Great." He traveled around the country performing his magic in front of large audiences.

By the late 1880s, Mary Eliza Woodruff Bell purchased the house. She was the widow of Colonel Samuel Bell, a Confederate officer, and brought her daughters with her to live at Curran Hall. Her granddaughter Averell Tate was born in the house and she eventually inherited it from her aunt.

Alden Woodruff, a brother of Bell, was renting from his sister while his own house was being repaired after a fire. During his stay, he became aware of a ghost and believed it to be Mary Walters. He was so convinced that she existed that he painted the beautiful cypress floors and plaster walls black in hopes of seeing her against a dark color.

Woodruff was desperate to communicate with her. Bell discovered what he had done after a visit and was upset to find her house in such disarray. She asked Woodruff to leave immediately, and once he had done so, she and her daughters moved back, where she remained until her death in 1911.

Bell's granddaughter Averell Tate was an adult with her own family by the time she inherited the house. She and her husband raised their two children at Curran Hall, and she remained there until her husband's death and the children were grown and out on their own. The house became the Little Rock Visitor Center years later.

Tate loved the house; it was a part of her from the time she was born. People close to her loved to hear stories about the legends and myths surrounding the history of the place, and she loved to talk about it.

There was a story about a ghost that occupied the house—one of the tales she liked to talk about. She also remembered a place in the floor located in a corner of the front parlor that looked similar to a trapdoor—perhaps the stories about Frolich were true after all.

When Tate was a teenager, she had already spent most of her life at Curran Hall and loved to go ghost-hunting in the neighborhood every Halloween with her friends. She said she never personally encountered a ghost herself while in the house but she did notice some unexplained, spooky things that happened through the years.

When someone died, for instance, visitation time with family and friends was the night before the funeral. This gave people a chance to come by and pay their respects. The coffin of the deceased was on display in the main parlor of the house. At Curran Hall, this setup was located in the front parlor by the big set of doors separating that room from the dining room or in front of the fireplace. Tate always thought her cats and dogs knew that because they would never lie down in these two locations.

Cats are fascinated with death, and some believe that they are attracted to the flesh of the deceased. For many years, stories have been told about cats circling a house when a death occurs. Felines seem to have a natural mystique about them anyway, so it's easy to accept this belief as fact, especially when people relate the story over and over again.

Curran Hall once had a resident cat that lived on the premises. His name was Scout, and a mysterious-looking woman would come to feed him on the corner of the property. A shed in the backyard provided shelter for him, and he was often seen crawling under the foundation. His caretaker was very private and didn't care to talk to anyone.

With stories and sightings about the ghosts who haunt the house, a resident cat added to the mystery of it all. When I was an employee of the visitor

The shed at Curran Hall is located in the backyard and was used as an office by Colonel Ebenezer Walters. Years later, another owner attached it to the main house and used it for a bedroom and bath. *Photo by David Hoge.*

center, I attempted to ask the mysterious woman about the cat. Reluctantly, she told me the story.

The cat was born on the property seventeen years previously and was the guardian of Curran Hall. It was his job to watch over the place, and she had been taking care of him all that time and was his protector. So, what do you say after that explanation?

A few years after this encounter, Scout was attacked by some dogs and died from his wounds. The distraught caretaker came to tell me what had happened and later wrote a nice card thanking me for allowing her and Scout to stay around the house. A few days later, after this episode, some people who knew her said she became ill and disappeared—never to be seen again.

Curran Hall was built almost two centuries ago, and even today, people talk about the ghost(s) who occupy the place. In 2002, after it reopened as the visitor center, a young woman who lived across the street remarked that at night she could see something through the windows moving around inside the house.

Sometimes, the image appeared to be a woman walking back and forth, but the young woman across the street never saw her looking out the window.

The neighbor initially thought it to be someone who worked there, but considering that the occurrences took place after-hours, she knew the image couldn't be an employee.

One day, I was approached by a visitor who could see spirits. He told me that I was being followed by a young woman dressed in nineteenth-century attire and that her name was Mary Eliza. Two women by that name were associated with the house, and I explained who they were.

I showed him a picture of the older Mary Eliza Bell that was hanging in the parlor, but he said she was older than the spirit following me. I told him the story of Mary Eliza Walters, the original owner who died before living in the house. He confirmed that she was the spirit. I didn't realize it at the time, but I was about to experience some paranormal activity.

About that time, unusual and unexplained things began to happen, and the staff and I were wondering what was going on. One night after an event, we were cleaning up when the commercial coffee maker, already turned off for the night, began hissing and producing steam that sounded like an old railroad steam engine.

Coffee dripped into the carafe—what appeared to be an impossible task was happening before our very eyes. We couldn't believe what we were seeing; coffee being made with neither water in the reservoir nor coffee grounds in the basket. We had to unplug the unit in order to get it to stop.

Unexplained events continued to happen, such as a rocking chair rocking by itself on the porch and a glass bottle moving back and forth inside the curio cabinet. A picture was thrust to the floor from its location on the wall with such force that the glass shattered into pieces.

Also, numerous false security alarms were triggered by "something" in the shed. Another employee sighted a man dressed in a Civil War uniform sitting in one of the dining room chairs. Visitors sensitive to the paranormal have mentioned cold spots, an unusual feeling or a presence in a certain location of the house. One visitor remarked about feeling the presence of someone in one of the rocking chairs.

On one occasion, during an outdoor wedding, the door to the shed slowly opened with the greatest of ease—a feat not normally possible since the floor is uneven and the door sticks along the way. One night, a shadowy figure was observed as it moved across the mantle on the dining room fireplace.

All of this paranormal excitement gave us cause to find out who might be haunting the house. After several investigations, we found out it was Mary Walters and Averell Tate, both of whom have left voices on recorders. Mary's voice was especially haunting as she said in a whisper, "Mary, that's who I am."

The grandfather clock in the parlor of Curran Hall mysteriously started running after I gave notice that I was leaving. It kept perfect time and chimed on each hour for the remaining two weeks I was there. Today, it stands quietly just as before. *Photo by David Hoge.*

Tate was the last private owner and moved out of the house when it became too cumbersome for her to take care of. The city of Little Rock bought it in 1996 and, along with a group of well-meaning people, made plans to save it.

They felt it was historically important and embarked on a mission of raising money and tackling the massive overgrowth of shrubs and vines, thus transforming it into the beautiful Little Rock Visitor Center. It was a six-year project, and everyone met the task with enthusiasm and pride.

In 2002, the house opened its doors and since then, it has welcomed thousands of people from all over the world. It is a peaceful place, and one is drawn to the rocking chairs on the porch. Many a tired traveler has taken the time to rock their stresses away from their journey.

Listening to the birds chirp in the surrounding trees and gardens adds to the experience. Although it is haunted and has a few resident ghosts, it is truly a beautiful building, restored to the likeness of its earlier days.

The time had come for me to leave Curran Hall and begin a new adventure. I told the staff my plans and gave my notice. I walked into the parlor and glanced over at the grandfather clock. It began to chime and run. I was mesmerized—the staff had not been able to get it to work since it was placed in the house—yet now it was running.

I continued to work for the next two weeks, and the clock continued to run, surprisingly chiming on the hour. My final day arrived, and as I turned to close the door for the last time, the clock stopped and hasn't worked since.

The Little Rock Visitor Center is a beautiful and serene place to visit. If you get the chance, stop by and sit in one of the rockers. Close your eyes, and listen to the sounds around you. Perhaps Averell will sit in an adjoining rocker, Scout will rub against your leg or Mary will whisper softly in your ear, "Mary, that's who I am." Then you will know that you have been welcomed by the spirits who occupy Curran Hall.

CHAPTER 2

The Tower Building at the Little Rock Arsenal

One of the most haunted places in the South is the building that houses the MacArthur Museum of Arkansas Military History. Once known as the Tower Building at the Little Rock Arsenal, it is today home to a variety of military-related exhibits.

The museum opened its doors on May 19, 2001, for the primary purpose of displaying military artifacts. Arkansas, and specifically Little Rock, has a proud military heritage and is fortunate that pieces of the past are viewed in such an environment, because the building itself is a major part of our military history.

The Tower Building was built in 1840 and was one of several buildings that comprised the Little Rock Arsenal. According to the director of the museum: "By 1855, the arsenal had been designated as a Class 3 'Arsenal of Deposit' under the control of the U.S. Army's Ordnance Department," and it was one of the richest depositories in the United States.

The primary purpose of the arsenal's existence was to house ammunition and weapons for local militia in case of mobilization. The Capital Guards were Little Rock's militia company and kept their own weapons and armory in their basement headquarters near the intersection of Markham and Main streets.

During the Civil War, the Little Rock Arsenal was occupied by the Confederate and Union armies, at separate times, of course. You might think that with that much firepower on hand, surely an accident might have happened that caused a death or two, but historians are adamant that no one died in the building's long history.

The Tower Building, once part of the Little Rock Arsenal, is the birthplace of General Douglas MacArthur. Known as one of the most haunted places in the South, it stands today as the MacArthur Museum of Arkansas Military History. *Photo by David Hoge.*

There is evidence from paranormal investigations that something ghostly is going on. Many have reported cold spots, sightings of apparitions and voices heard through digital recorders and in person. So is it fair to say that a place can be haunted without a death occurring? Of course, as a spirit haunts where they have a connection, and that connection can be anything from a person to a piece of furniture.

Who could be haunting the Tower Building? Let's go back to the beginning, when Arkansas was about to become a state. Changes were in our future as we evolved from a territory on the edge of the frontier to statehood.

Arkansas' population had grown, and the territory met the criteria for becoming a state. The time came to begin the application process, but it was met with opposition because Arkansas was a slave state. Congress didn't want additional slave states admitted to the Union. According to the Missouri Compromise of 1820, a slave state could apply for statehood as long as a free state also applied at the same time. Michigan was a free state and was admitted six months after Arkansas.

In the summer of 1836, the Arkansas Territory became the twenty-fifth state to join the United States of America. Because Arkansas was a slave state, that designation would play a part in the future of American history. Little Rock had been the territorial capital since 1821, so it was a natural transition for the city to become the capital of the new state. As the seat of government, and being centrally located, citizens would find it convenient to conduct state business here.

Arkansas' citizens were guaranteed the same rights as those in other states. They could elect state officials and vote in presidential elections. Arkansas had representation in Congress and was able to have political parties.

The first Arkansas governor was James Sevier Conway, and when Arkansas became a state, he requested that the federal government build an arsenal to stockpile ammunition and weapons. Everyone was concerned that there might be an attack from Native Americans.

Arkansas was on the edge of the frontier in 1836, and some people thought of Arkansas as an Indian state because of its geographic location. The state initially was part of the Missouri Territory and encompassed the land known today as the state of Oklahoma, which was the newly established Indian Territory.

In fact, Arkansas was a thoroughfare for the Native Americans as they traveled west to Oklahoma. They came from their homeland in the east and carried whatever they could manage. Several routes were designated for this passage, and thousands migrated during the Indian Relocation Movement, commonly known as the Trail of Tears. You will read more about this topic in other chapters in this book.

This journey was inhumane and very difficult for the Native Americans. Walking was the only way most of them traveled, but others came by horse and wagon. The tribal leaders and their families came aboard boats and used the Arkansas River as the way to navigate to their new home. Many died along the way, and some of these deaths were in our state.

Arkansas was occupied by the Quapaw Indians before the white man came and settled. Cherokee, Muscogee, Seminole, Chickasaw and Choctaw were the tribes making their way to Oklahoma and were known as the Five Civilized Tribes.

Little Rock's citizens were grateful that construction of the arsenal was approved and immediately felt secure knowing they would now be protected. The job of finding an appropriate spot fell on Major Robert B. Lee of the U.S. Army (apparently no relation to the better-known Robert E. Lee.) Major Lee looked over several pieces of land and settled on thirty-six acres on the outskirts of town. It was a familiar place to the locals because the Little Rock Jockey Club used it for its racetrack.

The track was built around 1834 by a small group of local citizens who wanted to race their horses and use the occasion for socializing. Once they found the amount of acreage that would accommodate a track, the construction process began. According to newspaper reports, "the races were action packed and full of boasting and bravado of the competing horse owners." But this communal activity only lasted a few years.

Construction began on the Tower Building around 1840, several years after Arkansas became a state. Lumber used for the framing came from trees

The Tower Building was built in 1840 for the primary purpose of storing ammunition and weapons. It was part of the Little Rock Arsenal for years and today is the MacArthur Museum of Arkansas Military History. Exhibits displayed are relevant to the wars Arkansans fought in. *Photo by David Hoge.*

near Pine Bluff, about sixty miles southeast of Little Rock. Stone and rock came from the north side of the Arkansas River in an area called "big rock quarry." Bricks made locally were also used. The arsenal is a fine, sturdy structure and has withstood the test of time.

According to *The Encyclopedia of Arkansas History and Culture*, when construction was completed, the *Arkansas Gazette* declared it to be "a splendid specimen of masonry." The Little Rock Arsenal was unique in that it had a center Tower Building, named for its octagon tower. During the next ten years, more than thirty buildings were added to the installation.

After the Mexican-American War ended in 1848, the remaining weapons were stored at the arsenal. Some of these would be used in the War Between the States, better known as the Civil War.

By 1860, trouble was brewing between the Northern states and the Southern "slave" states. Arkansas was in a sensitive position because it was a slave state, and the Little Rock Arsenal was manned by the federal government.

This situation quickly became a volatile issue that would lead to a confrontation. In fact, the Civil War almost started in Arkansas months before it began in South Carolina. Had it not been for the action of Captain James Totten, who was in charge of the federal troops at the arsenal, a skirmish might have occurred.

In February 1861, two months before the start of the Civil War, Captain Totten arrived at the arsenal with seventy-five U.S. troops. Up until that time, there had been a small group of federal soldiers guarding it. Rumors of secession were spreading like wildfire across the nation with speculation about which state would secede.

While waiting for a special state election to determine whether or not Arkansas would secede, approximately one thousand armed men from the southern and eastern part of the state arrived in Little Rock. Arkansas now faced a crisis because the angry crowd demanded that the arsenal turn over the weapons and surrender the building.

Governor Henry Rector called for the removal of the federal troops. Several attempts were made by Captain Totten to contact his superiors about what to do, but to no avail. They never responded to his messages, so he made the decision to leave Little Rock and avoid "the effusion of blood." Through his wisdom, the troops left the city and a conflict was avoided.

Two months later, citizens voted to secede from the Union. Arkansas joined the Confederacy and was no longer part of the federal government. The Confederate army had control of the arsenal for two years before Union troops marched in and seized the city in 1863.

Before the Union forces arrived, rumors indicated they were on the outskirts of town. Based on this information, state leaders packed what they needed from the state capitol building (now known as the Old State House) and moved state government to Old Washington in Hempstead County in the southwest corner of the state.

From the end of the war until 1890 when it was decommissioned, the Tower Building was renovated and became a housing complex for young officers and their families. It was no longer needed as a weapon depository.

The exterior view today is reflective of the changes made during the makeover. The porches and stairways were added to allow the families easy access to their quarters. The three-story building was converted into four apartments. The only entry into the building initially was through the basement on the backside where the stone arch is located. The arch is still visible today and used only by museum staff.

The interior was dramatically changed. Initially the three levels were open, as is typical of a warehouse. Access to the levels was by a platform lift and winding stairway, both located in the octagon tower. Remnants of the stairway are still there, but the lift was removed and today, a modern elevator is used by visitors to gain access to the second floor.

Interior walls were added to separate the individual apartments and establish a floor plan. A grand staircase in the center of the building was constructed to aid residents going to their quarters on the second floor.

This staircase is a hot spot for spirits. Photos reveal orbs and misty areas in this location. At the top of the grand staircase is a landing where the apparition of a woman has been seen.

A photo taken of me while addressing the haunted tour group revealed an orb near my face. My tours meet at this location, and it's a great way to start the journey.

The building is dark with light only in a few areas. The group waits at the base of the grand staircase for my arrival. I'm on the second floor waiting for my cue, and I can hear the conversations taking place below. Comments such as:

"Did you see that dark image move over there!"

"I just heard someone whisper in my ear!"

"Look, over there, something was moving in the dark!"

One woman was so scared that she said she was going to have a heart attack.

The history of the building has been covered in this chapter, but the issue of why it's haunted has not been resolved. Several events related to death have occurred on the grounds. Little Rock's first autopsy was performed in

The grand staircase on the first floor of the MacArthur Museum of Arkansas Military History was built in the late 1800s. It was part of the remodeling effort converting the Tower Building into temporary housing quarters for young, married officers and their families. *Photo by David Hoge.*

the back of the building. David O. Dodd, a seventeen-year-old, was hanged nearby because he was found guilty of being a Confederate spy.

Yellow Fever was in epidemic proportions during the Civil War. Many of the soldiers died during this time as a result. A local psychic who surveyed the Tower Building said that she saw two Confederate soldiers arguing in the basement. A black laundress was seen as she walked from room to room carrying a basket full of clothes at the base of the grand staircase. Soldiers sick with the fever lay on cots in the basement. The psychic said people died in the building, a statement that totally contradicts what the historians believe.

The Tower Building is a paranormal's haven. The staff is generous about allowing groups to spend hours walking around in the dark with their equipment. The floors are creaky, but otherwise there is dead silence and sounds are easily picked up on recording equipment. (The silence is broken when the fire trucks at the station across the street leave with blaring sirens.)

The basement area is what gives everyone a chill and fright. No one likes to be down there alone.

From 1942 until 1997, the Museum of Natural History and Antiquities occupied the building. A distant aunt of mine, Bernie Babcock, founded the museum in 1927, and before it relocated here, it previously occupied the third floor at Little Rock City Hall.

Mrs. Babcock influenced city leaders into letting her relocate the museum to the then-vacant Tower Building. The arsenal had long ago been removed, and the buildings were either torn down or sold. The only building left standing was the Tower Building, and it was vacant. The surrounding area was the location of a new city park and a museum of this stature would be the highlight.

She was a firm believer in the afterlife and communicating with spirits. A participant in séances, she loved getting things stirred up and lived in the basement of the building while setting up her museum. Like most basements, this one is underground and made of stone. One has the feeling of being in a cavern, and it's hard to imagine that someone could sleep there. Mrs. Babcock was a distinguished author and the first Arkansas woman to be included in *Authors and Writers Who's Who*.

She also had another side that made her a very interesting woman. She was a spiritualist and wanted to contact Abraham Lincoln and Ann Rutledge through séances. Mrs. Babcock loved history and enjoyed reading and researching young Abe Lincoln and his first love, Ann Rutledge.

Several séances were held in the museum as a result of her beliefs. Perhaps she felt cold spots or saw the unusual images that are experienced today. Perhaps these spiritual events are the remnants of her séances. She was known to travel around the country taking part in others. Her beliefs and acceptance of the afterlife came from her mother. The following is an observation made at her mother's deathbed:

> *Mom's great desire and prayer for years was that she might live to see her children all grown, and this she did. When she finished this earthly existence all six children and husband were grouped around her bed to kiss her the last farewell. None feared for the hereafter of the soul of such a mother. Shortly before consciousness left she said: "Now children, you know we have many times wondered about spiritualism, and whether it is possible for a spirit to return to commune with those still on this plane of life; now I am going; I shall soon know; and always remember this: If it is possible for this to happen, depend upon it, I shall come to you direct, never thru some stranger who may claim to have a message for you from your mother." She spoke of her passing as going on a journey; soon she would join her father and mother; she wished us to be happy for her and then she feel into eternal sleep.*

The topic of whether the Tower Building is haunted by spirits will continue to be a subject of conversation for years to come. Some think it a novel idea but not a possibility. But on the other side, the spiritualists think the building has ghosts from top to bottom. What do you think? The answer is up to the individual and can only be determined by him or her. Visit the museum, stand at the base of the grand staircase and see what happens. Or go to the second floor, walk into the theater, sit in the dark and see if you can hear the voice that others have heard.

What does the voice say?

"Get out!"

CHAPTER 3

THE EMPRESS OF LITTLE ROCK

One of the grandest homes in Little Rock is a Queen Anne–style masterpiece, a true example of Victorian design whose turrets and towers rise to the heavens on the corner of Twenty-second and Louisiana. The house is so commanding in appearance that it conjures up an eerie feeling to the onlooker. The gothic style lends to the haunted look as well.

Because of events that have taken place over the years, the current owners, as well as others, believe that the spirit of James Hornibrook occupies the house. He was the original owner and built it for his wife and five children. Located just four blocks from the Arkansas Governor's Mansion, it is in the boundaries of the Quapaw Quarter and specifically the Governor's Mansion Historic District—an upscale downtown neighborhood.

Today, the house is known as the Empress of Little Rock Bed and Breakfast, but before it became one of the top B&B's in the country, it was the historic Hornibrook House. James and Margaret, along with their children, moved from Toronto, Canada, to Little Rock in 1867.

The Hornibrooks left family and friends behind in Canada and began a new life in a Southern state that was scarred from the Civil War. Arkansans were struggling to regain control of their lives and heal their physical, emotional and financial wounds. Reconstruction was a slow process.

Little Rock's citizens looked upon all Northerners as carpetbaggers—whether or not they were. The term "carpetbagger" came from the perception that these people moving from the North carried their possessions in luggage made from

The Empress of Little Rock Bed and Breakfast located in the historic Hornibrook House. Built in the late 1800s, it is a fine example of Queen Anne Victorian architecture. *Photo by David Hoge.*

carpet. Many caused problems for the Southerners by trying to gain control of land, businesses and government—truly taking advantage of a horrific situation.

During the Civil War, there was a time when Arkansas was occupied by Union forces. Arkansans were denied ownership of weapons, could not own a liquor license and could not enter certain business areas. Into this economic climate came Mr. Hornibrook from out of the country with money he received from his family. He opened a saloon, and this business venture enabled him to become one of the richest men in the state.

But all the money in the world cannot buy happiness. Little Rock's society would not accept Hornibrook and his family. His flamboyant lifestyle didn't help his image, either.

In the mid-1800s, wealthy men were building impressive homes for their families. Several local men were making money and beginning to live the good life. Scott Street was a popular avenue for settling down and working. In fact, it was referred to as the "Main Street" of Little Rock during this time.

Hornibrook's archrival was Angelo Marré, another saloon owner. However, unlike Hornibrook, Marré was accepted into local society which approved of him building his home on the popular residential street. Marré's wife, Jenny, and their children lived in the Villa Marré until his death. Jenny moved from the house after her remarriage. (From 1986 to 1993, the Villa Marré was used in the opening scenes of the television comedy show *Designing Women*.)

Hornibrook wanted to build a beautiful home to express the love he felt for his wife; money was no object to him and only the best would do. He searched for land on what was then the outskirts of town, knowing he wouldn't be welcomed elsewhere. Accepting his dilemma, he acquired some acreage and began to make plans for the house.

In 1882, he engaged architects Kasper Kusner and Max Orlopp, who were thought to be personal friends of his family. The Hornibrooks and the architects drafted the blueprints for the house. The cost of constructing the enormous 7,200-square-foot house was reported to be $20,000 at a time when a home of normal size would run between $2,500 and $3,500.

Hornibrook requested that Arkansas materials be used throughout the house. Native woods such as oak, cherry, walnut, mahogany, cypress and yellow pine were used in the wainscoting and parquet floors. Geometric room designs of circles, squares and octagons were incorporated into the floor arrangement, making the floor patterns a unique feature.

Other natural materials used were rock, granite, limestone, quartz and crystal. Bricks and stucco were also used in the construction. In addition to his saloon, Hornibrook was vice-president of Edison Electric. Being in this position, he was aware of the latest technology and was inspired to use it throughout the house. For instance, he installed an intercom system that proved valuable when calling the family together. Heating came from steam, but the house also had six fireplaces and three water closets, with bathtubs and running hot water.

The historic James Hornibrook house is the location of the Empress of Little Rock Bed and Breakfast. Built in the late 1800s, the house today is one of the finest examples of Victorian design and is considered a Queen Anne–style masterpiece. *Photo by David Hoge.*

On the second-floor landing, an eight-foot-square stained-glass skylight was built—another unique feature to the house and one requiring a phenomenal foundation to support it because of its enormous size. By 1888, the house was finished and the family moved in and began enjoying their new home.

The *Arkansas Gazette* announced that "A Handsome Residence" had been built for $20,000 at Twenty-second and Louisiana and would be "one of the finest residences in the state." The following year, another article appeared in the newspaper announcing that the Hornibrook House was "one of the most important buildings constructed in Little Rock in 1888."

Twenty-one years had slipped by since their arrival in Little Rock, but life doesn't always remain the same, and two years after moving into their new home, tragedy struck. On May 24, 1890, Hornibrook had spent most of the day with his family and after supper left for his saloon to join friends.

Around 3:00 a.m., he left for home on the streetcar with three neighbors. One of the men accompanied Hornibrook to the front gate and left after saying goodnight. It was then that Hornibrook suffered an "apoplectic" stroke and fell to the ground, striking his head on the walk.

This type of stroke is caused by an interruption of the blood supply to the brain by rupture or obstruction of an artery. In other words, a clot may have formed and lodged in an artery. A delivery boy discovered his body and told the family. His youngest daughter, Maggie, realized her father had died and carried his body to the front porch. He was only forty-nine and in his prime.

A few years later his beloved wife, Margaret, died—reportedly from a broken heart. They are buried together in Mount Holly Cemetery, and a marble mask Hornibrook had made of himself while traveling to Italy is mounted on his gravestone. Their children inherited the estate, and daughter Lessie and her husband lived in the house and took care of the other children.

As time passed, the house changed hands. In 1897, the Arkansas Women's College leased it, and the school remained there for several years. It was then sold to Colonel and Mrs. Asbury Fowler in the early 1900s and once again became a private residence.

Fowler was an insurance agent for the Massachusetts Mutual Life Insurance Company. He left the insurance business and served as a federal marshal for four years and continued to live in the house until his death in 1922. Mrs. Fowler remained in the house until the Great Depression hit but was forced to give up her home and move to a much smaller house around 1930. According to the city directory, it was vacant from that time until 1938.

It became a boardinghouse in the next chapter of its existence. During World War II, a munitions plant was operating in nearby Jacksonville, northeast of Little Rock. Women were the major employees because the men who would have been working in the factory were instead off fighting overseas. These female workers were housed all over the county, and so the Hornibrook house became a place to board.

Stories have been told by these former residents about their boyfriends "calling on them" and how much they enjoyed sitting on the wrap-around front porch. Even then, the house must have been beautiful to those young ladies and their friends.

Fast forward about fifty years to 1993, when Bob Blair and Sharon Welch-Blair achieved their dream and purchased the house. It had been more than one hundred years since the house was built, and the Blairs were just as excited as the Hornibrooks must have been to be moving in. Both families knew they needed to take care of the place and create not only a home but also a showplace.

The Hornibrooks were fortunate to be the first family to move in, but the Blairs are credited for returning it to its original state. There were many owners in between, and all of them used it for different purposes. The new owners loved the house as soon as they saw it and envisioned returning it to the elegant Victorian style they had always loved.

So much had to be done, and it would take funding and time to return the house to the "grand ole lady" she once was. The house came not only with untold memories but also, apparently, a few ghosts.

The first story of a haunting begins about a year after the Blairs bought the house, during the process of reconstruction and restoration. The story told to me by Mr. Blair was that he was near the grand staircase on the first floor.

> *As I stood in the midst of a dark dreary kitchen, ready to be demolished, an apparition of a handsomely dressed man in a dapper Homburg hat descended the stairwell in a floating fashion. His eyes were peering beneath the hat. His clothes matched and were elegant and crisp. We gazed at each other and the hair on my neck was raised. I couldn't get his eyes out of my mind—they were haunting. His glance seemed to plead "Save this house."*

A short time after that first encounter, Mr. Blair experienced another when an arctic cold rush of wind brushed against him. This time, he was standing in the foyer, and all windows and doors were closed in the house.

The tower, with multiple glass panes, was known as the card room and located in the attic. Accessible by a narrow stairway, it was the gathering place for James Hornibrook and his friends to play cards in the invitation–only game. *Photo by David Hoge.*

He knew the cold air he felt could not have been a draft. This sensation is hard to explain but when the cold wind was near him, he felt that someone was saying, "Don't dare forget whose house this is. I'm watching."

The renovation was far enough along that bed-and-breakfast guests were now able to come and stay the night. Some minor painting and staining was still necessary to finish the massive project. A contract painter was working on the finishing touches. He had been up in the attic where the infamous card room was located—a small room to one side of the large attic.

He ran out of stain and left to get more on the other side of the attic. When he returned to the room, the door was locked and at that time had no key. Unable to open the door, he went to get a screwdriver but on his return found the door open and the ghostly figure of a finely dressed man wearing a Homburg hat. He ran from the attic, passing Mr. Blair on the first floor, and said he was never coming back.

The card room is a mystical area located above the front of the house. A separate flight of narrow stairs leads you to the entrance of the large attic from the second-floor landing. Once there, you walk across the boarded floor to the other side, where you'll find the small room that Hornibrook had built to be used for his private gambling parties.

Hornibrook's visitors used the servants' entrance and stairs and then would climb the steep attic stairs from the second-floor landing. This private game was invitation only, and the invitation was highly prized. This is the room that seems the most haunted. Furniture is turned over, faint laughter is heard and the odor of cigar smoke can be smelled. A visitor to the B&B can pick up on the goings on if staying in one of the bedrooms below the card room.

Guests of the Empress are excited about sharing their experiences, and the following is an account of one of those guests, as told to the innkeeper. The event happened in the summer of 1997:

> *"The souls are still here," she said. The first sighting was just outside her room. There standing was a large woman, dressed in pink, with her hair up on her head. The woman was wearing a lace scarf around her neck and appeared to be about 30–35 years old. Later that evening, the guest looked in another room. It was very cold, dark and smelled of pipes or cigars. There she saw a man that appeared to be a captain. He was angry or perhaps drunk. The captain was a heavy set man, with a white beard, black pants, white shirt, and tall black boots. Hanging on the back of a chair in the room was a military or maritime style coat with gold buttons and eyelets. On the bed, was a slim little woman that seemed to be crying or upset? In what is now known as the maids' closet, the guest found a young black woman folding laundry. To her the closet seemed damp and colder compared to the room where she saw the captain. It also had the smell of "old." All through the night she heard men's voices above her laughing, children arguing, and sounds of boots stomping or occasionally canes hitting the floor. It lasted until around 4:00 a.m. and then the house became dead quiet. It was then she could feel someone looking at her from above.*

It is assumed that the people she saw were ghosts, since she was the only person in the house at the time.

A woman from Maryland who visits Little Rock every month on business wanted to take the local haunted tour of the city and asked if the Empress was on the tour schedule. After receiving confirmation that it was, she joined the group and told her story about her overnight visits and the paranormal experience she had in the B&B. Here is a portion of her story as told to the tourists while on the haunted tour.

> *I fell into a light twilight sleep with my light on. I was in the small bedroom that faces the top of the stairs. A shadow appears and blocks the light, I sit up, look around, but nothing is there. I lie back down, shut my eyes, and the shadow appears again blocking the light. I am fully awake now but afraid to open my eyes. I can feel a male standing next to the bed, blocking my light. I speak out loud and say, "I know that someone is here. But I would appreciate it if you would let me be to get some sleep. I have to get up early, and I need my rest. Thanks for letting me know that you are here." It left, and the light was in view again. The following couple of nights, I spoke to it before I went to sleep, and it left me alone. Though when I would come into the house, I always said hello and felt like someone was home though I knew no one was there but me most of the time. The housekeeper told me that some guests had seen a man in Victorian garb.*

The Empress has received multiple awards both locally and nationally as an accommodations and event facility. The essence of a more romantic era is captured during a stay, but the staff and facility are prepared to meet the needs of modern-day travelers, business guests and brides.

With high-end spa amenities available, it offers packages designed to relax guests in the privacy of the Victorian sanctuary. It was named the "Fourth Most Romantic B&B in the United States" by *Country Almanac* magazine and one of the Top Ten "Best of the South" Category by BedandBreakfast.com

Upon entering the Grand Sitting Parlor, you immediately notice the wonderful fragrance of something cooking in the kitchen or other aromatic flavors. A relaxing mood takes over, and you want to lie down somewhere peaceful—perhaps the hammock in the Moonlight Secret Garden would be satisfying. The vintage quartz fountain makes a pleasant sound as the water trickles—it can put you to sleep.

The Empress of Little Rock will leave an impression that you will always remember. That's why guests keep returning year after year, and it is consoling to know that perhaps Mr. Hornibrook is watching over you.

CHAPTER 4
PAUL'S HOUSE

On a cold January night in 2011, a security guard at Parris Towers made his final round just before his shift ended. It was midnight, and as he walked to his car, he scanned the building, grounds and neighborhood.

Parris Towers, an apartment building, is located between Broadway and Arch Street in Little Rock's Quapaw Quarter Historic District. As the guard's eyes glanced toward homes across the street, he noticed the flicker of flames on the side of one house. The fire grew in intensity, and the guard immediately ran to the house to alert the occupants.

By the time he reached the front porch, some of the neighbors also began to run toward the house and, in the distance, he could hear sirens from approaching fire trucks and other emergency vehicles.

He knocked repeatedly on the front door as he shouted, "Fire! Wake up!" The sleeping young couple who lived in the house quickly awoke to the voices of the security guard and other bystanders who were chiming in.

The couple quickly ran from their first-floor bedroom into the living room to unlock the front door, where they were greeted by the security guard, firemen, neighbors and police. After an evaluation of the fire, authorities determined that the fire appeared to be on the outside of the chimney flue and in the attic.

This made for a very dangerous situation—the flames were only apparent on the outside of the house, not to the occupants inside. The blaze probably originated with a spark from a fire in the fireplace going through a small crack in the firebox, igniting timbers within the walls.

Above: The bungalow-style home where Paul Wallace and his wife, Bonny, lived before their untimely deaths. It was built in the late 1800s. *Photo by David Hoge.*

Right: This chimney on the side of Paul's house was the scene of an unusual fire that alarmed the occupants and neighbors. *Photo by David Hoge.*

The house was finally secured, and the young couple spent the night with neighbors. With dawn approaching, they fell asleep knowing that they'd have to spend the day looking for another place to live.

This wasn't the first time that something traumatic had taken place at this house on Arch Street. Luckily, no one died this time—although the same couldn't be said for other chapters in the house's history.

The house was built in 1886 by Butler, Gibb and Company and was to be used primarily as rental property. Seven years later, however, it was purchased by a couple, Mr. Edward Cornish and his wife, Winona, for their family's home. But tragedy struck the family two years later.

In June 1895, their young son, Joseph, just two years old, and daughter "Little Winona," age unknown, died just three days apart. The children are believed to be the first people to die in the house.

Tragedy struck once again on September 27, 1898. Just three years after losing his two small children, Cornish's loving wife, Winona, their newborn infant and little Ruth, age six, all died within hours of each other.

They were buried together in the same coffin next to the graves of Joseph and "Little Winona" at Mount Holly Cemetery in Little Rock. Now alone, Ed Cornish needed to find some way to carry on with his life. He eventually sold the house and immersed himself in his work.

Cornish, a prominent Arkansas banker for more than twenty-four years, was involved with all the banks of Little Rock at one time or another. During a major portion of that time, he headed the largest financial institution in Arkansas. As a member of Little Rock's high society, Cornish met and married Hilda Kahler of St. Louis, Missouri, and their union produced six children.

Edward and Hilda Cornish built a stately brick mansion with the best materials money could buy. The Cornish House was then and is today one of Little Rock's grandest homes. Ironically, the house is located just one block from the Arch Street house where he lived with first wife, Winona, and their children.

In early November 1928, Mr. Cornish ended his life in a downtown hotel in New Orleans. A preliminary police report stated that he killed himself with a shot through the temple, and his body was found slumped in a chair, still holding the .45-caliber automatic pistol. He left two farewell letters addressed to his wife, saying he was leaving his fortune to her alone, but gave no reason for the decision to take his life.

The coroner said that a binder containing his papers was found in his effects and suggested that Cornish had sustained financial upsets. Obviously, this came as a shock to poor Hilda, who by that time was a well-known woman who had made a name for herself as an advocate for birth control. She continued her work in this field and is credited with the founding of Planned Parenthood of Arkansas.

The house has been consistently occupied since its construction. By the mid-1970s, the owners divided it into a duplex, a common practice for some downtown properties. During this period of the house's history, another death occurred, but this time the victim did not die in the house.

The renters at the time were two women, believed to be nurses employed at one of the local hospitals. They were living in what was the back apartment, accessed by an entry on an adjoining street. A person entered through a pair of French doors upstairs that led to the bedroom/office area.

One day, two men, thought to be co-workers, came by for a social visit but apparently had more on their minds than idle chitchat. After raping the women at gunpoint, they shot each one in the head, leaving them for dead.

According to the police report, help arrived when the renters of the front apartment heard calls for help. They also heard the sound of someone beating on a shared wall coming from the back apartment.

Dorothy Mullen, one of the victims, never regained consciousness and died after being disconnected from life support. The other victim was saved by her braided hair. When she reached the hospital, she was unconscious and the surgeon assumed she had been shot in the head. While attempting to shave her hair for surgery, the bullet rolled onto the surgical table.

Apparently when the gun was fired, the bullet didn't penetrate her skull as suspected but became lodged in her thick, braided hair. She survived the ordeal and was able to identify and testify against the assailants. They were arrested and sentenced to serve time in prison.

Shortly after Dorothy Mullen died, Paul and Bonny Wallace purchased the house and planned to renovate the structure. They were historic preservation–minded people who saw potential in the house and wanted to take it from its duplex status back to a single-family dwelling.

The Wallaces decided to move downtown, where they could be closer to their jobs. They spent the next twenty-four years working on their house while making lifelong friends in the neighborhood.

Other renovations were taking place in historical buildings in the area; magnificent homes that had been divided into apartments, commercial businesses or homes for the elderly were now becoming showcases reminiscent of an era long forgotten. Such diverse architectural styles turned every avenue into a scenic route. But tragedy struck the Wallaces in August 2004, when a woman came knocking at the door one warm summer night.

The woman, who was renting a house from Bonny, stopped by to talk about a money issue. After a few hours, Paul was tired and went to bed, leaving Bonny and the woman still talking. It was shortly after midnight when he was awakened by gunshots. Paul discovered his wife had been shot and, although he was on oxygen for a medical condition, struggled with the woman when she pointed the weapon at him.

She squeezed the trigger twice at point-blank range, but the gun didn't fire. She then tried to suffocate him with a pillow. After her failed attempts to kill Paul, she ran off but was later arrested at her home.

Bonny Wallace was a respected researcher at the University of Arkansas for Medical Sciences, where she was director of clinical research for the Department of Surgery. Colleagues said she played a big role in pioneering and developing the hospital's burn unit and was most recently contributing to the development of new infrared imaging technology in the fight against breast cancer.

She had received numerous lifetime achievement awards for her work; her death was a loss to humanity. Her friends were devastated, but especially those from downtown, for those people living in the neighborhood bonded with each other and became like a family.

Paul continued to live in the house until his death from emphysema in October 2006, on the day of Bonny's birthday. During the time Paul and Bonny lived in the house, they sometimes heard strange noises and occasionally saw a glimpse of a spirit who appeared to be "a woman in a mint green dress." Paul saw the spirit again in the weeks before his death and took it as a sign that the end was near.

Paul's neighbor, who lived next door, cared for him after Bonny's death. He invited her and her family to stay with him while their nearby house was being remodeled. They were with him when he died and continued to live there until their house was finished.

One night, while the family was sleeping at Paul's house, an intruder broke into the house by removing a pane of glass from a French door that led to the outside. The intruder reached in and turned the key that was in the lock to let himself in. The intruder then wandered throughout the house.

One child was asleep on the living room couch, while the other was asleep in the front bedroom, areas that the intruder entered. The next morning when the family awoke to get ready for work and school, they discovered three laptop computers missing from inside the house as well as the family car outside. The keys had simply been picked up from the living room table.

It was upsetting to think that someone had been exploring the entire house while they slept, even opening the knife drawer in the kitchen. The outcome might have been very different if they had awakened during the intrusion.

The family feels to this day that something or someone kept them asleep during the time the perpetrator was in the Wallace's house, perhaps Paul's or Bonny's spirits. According to one of the children, apparitions of Bonny have been seen in her home next door.

In appreciation of the care he received, Wallace willed his estate to the neighbors who took care of him. They continued the Wallaces' dream of keeping the house as a single-family dwelling.

Their home was next door, which made it convenient for them to maintain both properties. They decided to use the Wallaces' house as rental property, and the young couple who were awakened by the fire that cold night in January were their first tenants.

From the time the couple moved in, strange things began to occur, and after initially passing the events off as "must be their imagination," they began to take notice and pay attention to the happenings. The names of Taylor, Tyler and Kyle were heard through whispered voices.

The bedrooms and surrounding area around these rooms seemed to be active with shadowy beings, described as the dark kind. For instance, the room they slept in had a pacing spirit, not malevolent, but it just paced back and forth. When getting up in the middle of the night to use the bathroom, they felt something that followed them and then "swooshed" past.

Friends experienced what felt like an arm reaching out and grabbing them; this sensation happened near the room where Bonny died. Most of their visitors freaked out when near the stairway.

People have commented when on the stairway about a strange feeling that overcomes them, but they cannot explain what the feeling is. The stairway is a hotspot for sensations of all kinds; others have mentioned a sensation similar to two hands pressing down on their shoulders when they come down from the second floor. It's described as feeling as though someone is pushing you down.

There are cold spots in the house that travel from room to room, but there are consistent spots in the two front rooms considered to be the original parlors. Sounds in the attic quieted down after removal of a personal item of Bonny's.

The attic sounds also eased after music was played—including band practice. A group of friends congregated at the house for their band practices. Some band members noticed unusual things going on, as did other friends

The backyard of Paul's house and the tree believed to be the site of paranormal events. *Photo by David Hoge.*

who frequented the house. Doors mysteriously unlocked after being locked. A friend who is sensitive to spiritual spots described his feeling as "taken aback" about something in the area around the big old tree in the backyard.

In fact, the couple, after carefully reviewing all the unexplained events inside and outside the house, wonder if the house was built on top of something that is causing the disturbances.

The house has been repaired since the fire, and the smell of new construction and paint is everywhere. It has an inviting characteristic to its appearance, which is apparent by the exterior harvest orange color that lures you to the front door.

You feel welcome when close by, a feeling as though you are home. Whatever is present in the house, whether spirit or otherwise, may or may not still linger there, but one thing is for sure; the house is ready and primed for the next occupants—no matter if they are human or ghostly.

CHAPTER 5
MOUNT HOLLY CEMETERY

One of the most popular tourist sites in Little Rock is located at the corner of Thirteenth Street and Broadway.

Mount Holly Cemetery is the city's oldest public cemetery and is the burial place for many of our state leaders. Governors, Civil War generals, state legislators and city mayors, along with other souls from all walks of life, are buried beneath the grass-covered graves.

It's been said that to walk through this cemetery is to walk through our state's history. The names on the grave markers are names we've heard all of our lives. Counties, schools, towns and such bear the names of some of those laid to rest here.

Mount Holly is located on a hill in the historic neighborhood called the Quapaw Quarter. The grassy pathways and park-like surroundings give the visitor the illusion of being in an earlier era. It's peaceful and quiet, which is remarkable because it's located next to an interstate and a busy street. Somehow the traffic sounds are muted while one is in the cemetery.

The foundation of Mount Holly in 1843 was preceded by three natural events that stirred up the citizens of Little Rock. In January 1843, an earthquake struck Little Rock. It was quite exciting, according to reports at the time. The jolting of the ground created enough force to cause items to fall from shelves.

Life in Little Rock was again disrupted by an act of nature when, at the end of January 1843, massive amounts of snow fell on the small community. The melting snow caused severe flooding.

Then, in February and March, people around the world saw an object in the sky that had many believing the end was near. The object was the Great March Comet of 1843, one of the largest and brightest comets ever recorded.

According to a book about the cemetery's history, *Jubilee: the First 150 Years of Mount Holly Cemetery*, "These unusual phenomena did not go unnoticed by Little Rock residents, and there were some predicting the world's end. Church attendance soared, and it is not too surprising to learn that a local Temperance Society was organized. It was enough to make any God-fearing person give thought to the uncertainties of life, death, and dying."

In that same year of these natural events, Chester Ashley and Roswell Beebe donated land to Little Rock for use as a public cemetery. Up until that time, burial grounds usually were in churchyards or one's own homestead. The need for a public site had been mandated by the Little Rock Town Council. Private cemeteries were banned, but the concept of a garden cemetery was on the horizon, thanks to the advent of Victorian-age cemeteries. They were becoming popular not only in Europe but also in our country.

The new cemetery style considered the grave site to be part of the family's estate and treated it as such. The grounds were secure within the perimeter of a wall made of stone or iron. They were well maintained and nicely landscaped, and the monuments were in a class comparable to sculpture. Symbolism was obvious throughout the area. A person's profession, religion or social status was chiseled into the stone with engraved text giving information about the deceased.

Monuments take on a different appearance at night, especially if the moon is full. The shadows and stillness of a cemetery contribute to a scary atmosphere. You can almost talk yourself into believing that something is moving and that sounds are being heard. Mount Holly is a stop on my tour of haunted places, and we enjoy our visits. Cameras snap pictures of misty images, orbs and other unexplainable objects. Some members of the tour groups have heard what sound like faint voices.

The cemetery is closed at night, so my tours are unable to enter the grounds after-hours. The Thirteenth Street gate is the only place outside the walls with a good view of the cemetery. As the group disembarks the tour bus, they gradually walk up to the gate with some hesitation. Once all are assembled, they stand next to the stone wall and peer through the iron gate. Soon cameras begin to flash as the tourists take pictures.

"Did you see what moved near that angel over there?" one person says. Or, "I just took a picture of a misty image by that urn," and then someone

The front gate of Little Rock's oldest public cemetery, Mount Holly. It was established in 1843 from land donated by two prominent citizens, Chester Ashley and Roswell Beebe. *Photo by David Hoge.*

says, "I just heard a soft voice whispering something in my ear and I could feel them close to my face."

One night, a unique picture was taken of a man who was on the tour. Another man's face also appeared in the picture. The picture was of two faces side by side, appearing to share one body. No one else in the group looked like the mystery man. Could it have been one of those "camera

Mount Holly Cemetery was established in 1843 for public burials, and this is a fine example of the sculptured grave markers that can be found there. A beautiful park-like setting makes this cemetery an inviting place to visit. *Photo by David Hoge.*

things?" Skeptics always think the equipment is the culprit, but those of us in the group that night knew differently!

The sexton is a cemetery employee who maintains the grounds, repairs the monuments and helps with funeral decisions. In the past, houses were built on the premises for him to live so he could be available at all times. Today, Mount Holly's sexton's cottage is used as a meeting place by the Mount Holly Cemetery Association. The sexton lives a few blocks from the cemetery.

Rumors from long ago say that past sextons were called on when passersby noticed movement in the cemetery at night and when a Mount Holly monument was found in a nearby neighbor's yard. Moving one of those monuments would be a challenging feat that a human couldn't do without the proper equipment!

After Ashley and Beebe donated the land, a picnic was held in May 1843 for people to mingle, eat and purchase a burial plot. Today, the annual Mount Holly Picnic is still a popular event, and folks gather to raise money for the cemetery's maintenance and upkeep.

Picnics have always been popular in the cemetery and have occurred through the years, but there was one picnic that was a little phenomenal. *Jubilee: The First 150 Years of Mount Holly Cemetery* shares a story first told by Fred W. Allsopp in his 1931 book, *Folklore of Romantic Arkansas*. Allsopp attributed the story to Judge Samuel W. Williams:

> *At a time when weekend diversions were few, park-like Mount Holly was a favorite gathering place on Sunday afternoons. It was on one such lazy Sunday afternoon that our story takes place. Arch Street ran through the middle of the cemetery at the time, and passersby on Eleventh or Thirteenth Streets could be readily seen by persons strolling on Arch Street.*
>
> *Looking up at the sound of hoof beats on Eleventh Street, a number of the promenaders recognized Robert Kincaid, dressed in a brown suit, soft hat, and blue shirt astride Nick, a horse that Kincaid had borrowed from the Williams family for a trip down to Saline County. They saw him—then he vanished into thin air. Those looking down Eleventh Street could see neither Robert nor the horse in either direction. The watch of one of the strollers pinpointed the time as 5:30 p.m.*
>
> *Williams returned home, expecting to see Robert and the horse, although it seemed much too soon for Robert to have ridden down to Saline County and returned. Robert was not at the house, Old Nick was not in the stable, and there was no evidence that either had returned. Williams' little daughter did not make the uneasy family feel any cheerier with her tearful insistence that Robert and Old Nick were dead.*

The following day a messenger rode in from Saline County and announced that Robert Kincaid had, in fact, been killed the day previous. When asked what time, they were told, "Yesterday at 5:30 p.m. he was riding by old man Ewan's, when Haws Ewan slipped into the orchard and shot him as he rode by. He filled him and his horse both with shot. As soon as some of us heard the shots, we hurried down the road, too late to save them. They were both dead." When asked what Robert had on, the messenger replied, "Brown suit, soft hat and blue shirt."

Though Williams had flair for telling a gripping story, be it fact or fiction, this was no fantasy. Others had shared the unnerving experience with him. What was the meaning of it all? We are left to ponder.

In 1877, the Mount Holly Cemetery Commission was formed to oversee the operation of Mount Holly. The commission was responsible for improving and beautifying the property in keeping with proper care for sacred ground. The commission changed Mount Holly's wilderness setting to a garden-like area. A stone wall was built to enclose the property, and maintenance of grave sites improved.

By 1884, by commission order, the remains of 600 to 640 Confederate soldiers were exhumed from Mount Holly and moved to Oakland Cemetery (near the National Cemetery). They were members of the Missouri, Arkansas, Texas and Louisiana Confederate commands. In a back corner of Oakland, the remains were buried in a semicircle, and a monument stands in the center. The headstones used at Mount Holly followed the soldiers to Oakland. Four Confederate generals and some other Civil War–era soldiers remain buried in Mount Holly.

David O. Dodd is one of the Confederate dead to be found in Mount Holly. He was hanged at age seventeen on a bitterly cold January day for being a Confederate spy. There has been an ongoing dispute about the spy story since the Civil War. Dodd was traveling back to his home in south Arkansas when he stopped at a Union army checkpoint. He had relinquished his travel pass earlier on arriving in Little Rock and didn't have another one.

During the search, he was found to be carrying coded information about the strength of the Union army in the Little Rock area. Although questioned intensely about where he got it, Dodd never divulged his source, and he was sentenced to hang as a Confederate spy.

Some believe he was protecting a young girl he had a crush on since he had just visited her home before returning to his family. Her father was known for entertaining the Union army officers, and some thought Dodd had managed to get the information while at her house. Every year on January 8, the anniversary of his 1864 death, a gathering of Confederate reenactors assemble at his grave site.

In the late 1800s, the *Little Rock Herald*, a local newspaper, reported that two prominent doctors were in the cemetery robbing graves. The news sent shockwaves throughout the medical community, which demanded to know the source of the information.

The doctors banded together and attempts to get the *Herald* to release the "libel source" were futile. This event resulted in a trial that didn't last long because the *Herald* editors admitted that they fabricated the story in order to have an exciting news day!

Mount Holly is a haven for master gardeners and others who enjoy a variety of trees, flowers and shrubs. The trees have grown to be quite large now and provide shady areas for the visitor to sit on the "cemetery furniture" while enjoying the peaceful setting. Mount Holly is one of the most beautiful cemeteries in the country.

This cemetery attracts birds and small animals because the area creates a natural setting for them. The layout of the property is typical of the Victorian-

The grave site of the Basham Daughters, whose physical representation was made of marble and believed to be sculpted in Italy. *Photo by David Hoge.*

age cemeteries. Horses and carriages were the modes of transportation in the cemetery's early days, so the pathways or lanes are narrow by today's standards. Automobiles are not able to drive easily throughout the cemetery, so parking outside is necessary.

Mount Holly has been referred to as the Westminster Abbey of Arkansas because of the number of prominent people buried there. An application was submitted for nomination to the National Register of Historic Places, and the cemetery received that honor on March 5, 1970. A notation on the application form stated that it was an "unaltered original site." The description said it was "quaint, imposing and inspiring with its funerary sculptures ranging from simple, traditional, chiseled stones of the mid-19th century to the ornate and grandiose monuments of the 1880-1890 periods." Mount Holly Cemetery stands among a small handful of cemeteries that carry this distinction of being on the National Register.

William B. Worthen Jr. said it best in the introduction he wrote for the *Jubilee* book. A portion of what he wrote:

> *Cemeteries speak to us. The rows and rows of graves remind us that we will follow—sooner or later—we will follow. The life-threatening disease, the auto accident, even the cry of the speeding ambulance, can give us the same message, but in a pushy, threatening way, like a rude intruder upon our sheltered lives.*
>
> *Cemeteries are gentle and so much more subtle. Clothed in park-like expanse, with foliage and monuments, death becomes an acquaintance who welcomes us to drop by before we come to stay. It is only at the funeral, or just thereafter, as the rough grave lies open to view, that the fragility of our lives also lies exposed and the graveyard seems unkind. Mount Holly contains history and has its own.*

The word "cemetery" comes from a Greek word meaning "sleeping chamber." During the nineteenth century, people were becoming more educated and sophisticated. The term "graveyard" was considered to be a coarse referral to burials. Death seems so final and permanent when the word "graveyard" is used. However, a "sleeping chamber" is soft and gentle. What reference sounds consoling to you?

Funerals still take place today in Mount Holly. As the onlookers stand before the grave, the cemetery's peacefulness takes hold. Comfort sets in, and you know, as the remains are lowered into the newly dug grave, that the deceased is merely "sleeping" until you meet again.

CHAPTER 6

TABORIAN HALL

Music faintly heard from an unknown source can make a person question his or her sanity. But when there is no logical explanation, do you suppose that it might be spiritual? Sounds unbelievable, but the possibility exists in the old Taborian Hall building located at 800 West Ninth Street.

In the mid-1900s, the building had the reputation of being the hottest place in town and was the location for some of the most popular African American entertainment attractions in the South. But long after its days of glory, it became an ugly sight to behold, all because of neglect.

Had it not been for Kerry McCoy, whose vision it was to create a future for this stately structure, it might have been demolished and its history lost forever. Taborian Hall is alive and well today, and the Dreamland Ballroom, located on the third and top floor of the hall, is once again a gathering spot for all ages. The room is rented for special events such as parties, fashion shows and a variety of musical performances.

In the late 1900s, Ms. McCoy was searching for a location to house her business, Arkansas Flag and Banner. She frequently drove downtown by way of Interstate 630 and noticed a grand old building on Ninth Street, north of the interstate and west of Broadway. Each time she made the trip; she was drawn to the building and knew that one day she'd have to go inside.

The day came for her visit, and as excited as she was to enter the building, she couldn't have imagined what she was about to see. Trash and debris were scattered everywhere. She had to cautiously navigate in between homeless people so as not to fall over them.

Then she reached the Dreamland Ballroom. She said, "The roof was missing, birds were flying around and the sun was illuminating the room. Staring across the open hole in the floor to the Dreamland stage and box seats, I had a feeling that was indescribable, a kind of euphoria."

That best describes what I also feel while in the building. You're mesmerized by it all. When inside, you see the exposed brick of the original structure; it's like looking into the building's past.

In addition to the ballroom, Taborian Hall once housed a variety of clubs in the early 1950s. There was one on each floor. Located in the basement was the Twin City Club; second floor was home to the Waiters Club; and Club Morocco was in the ballroom. Doc's Pool Hall occupied the first floor, and the scoreboards still have the scores from the last game played, although there's no way of telling how long ago that was.

The building has such character, and it is noticeable when first entering from the front door. The condition of the walls indicates that little, if anything has been done to sway from the original. Visitors to the building like the appearance and think it would be an injustice to modernize or update it.

Leaving it as close as possible to its original state is what gives the place its charm and mystique. The first time I entered the ballroom, I could feel something eerie around me. I'm not quite sure what the sensation was, but I accepted it and continued to walk around.

That's what you do the first time in the building, just walk around and stare at what's before you. The ballroom stage is obviously the center of attention because of its size, and you can just about imagine entertainers dancing and singing.

Ms. McCoy took over the building in 1991, and she began the process of cleanup and reconstruction. Soon Arkansas Flag and Banner moved into its new quarters and had room to stretch its legs, with plenty of extra space for future growth. As is obvious by its name, the business sells flags and banners and also makes custom banners for local, national and international individuals and businesses.

After moving into the building, some employees were on the second floor, where the offices and banner workshops are located. They heard swing music playing in the distance. They looked outside to see if anyone was on the street or in a car, but no one else was present. Another time, footsteps were heard on the third floor, as though people were walking in the unoccupied ballroom.

Doors have been heard slamming shut in other parts of the building when employees knew no one was there. Initially, anyone who heard the noises

Historic Taborian Hall is the home of Arkansas Flag and Banner. It is the only original building still standing in what was once Little Rock's African American business district. *Photo by David Hoge.*

was hesitant to tell others for fear he or she would be thought of as crazy. One day, when they were together, they heard a noise at the same time and then began to share their stories. Having their offices on the second floor is an ideal vantage point for observing what employees believe is a ghost or several ghosts.

Who could be haunting the building? There are several possibilities because of the age of the building and various activities that have taken place there over the years.

One well-known violent death was caused from a drive-by shooting that happened in front of Doc's Pool Hall. One of the owners, Black Mac, was shot while standing outside on the steps. Doc's was located on the ground floor of the original part of the building, and the clientele entered from the side street. He was hit by a hail shower of bullets coming from a car driving by. Remnants of the shooting are evident today by the bullet-chipped brick wall. Perhaps Black Mac is one spirit that haunts today.

The original building was constructed in the 1800s and was quite small, but it was destined to make its mark in history. In 1916, the Knights and Daughters of Tabor bought it with plans to expand the building. They were a religious organization, similar to the Freemasons, whose sole mission was

A side view of Taborian Hall, where Doc's Pool Hall was located years ago. A favorite hangout for African Americans at the time, it's also the scene of owner Black Mac's murder. *Photo by David Hoge.*

to "advance Christianity, education, morality and temperance—also, the art of governing, self reliance and true manhood and womanhood."

The organization offered sickness and burial insurance to the African American community, as well as a place to socialize. During the time they occupied the building, they supported the Taborian Hospital located in the neighboring state of Mississippi.

It took Simeon Johnson, a black contractor, two years to complete the remodeling, but the building was ready for occupancy and on its way to becoming an historical landmark. Initially known as Taborian Temple, the name was later changed to Taborian Hall. With the added space, black professionals were now able to offer services in a newly renovated building.

Black lawyers, dentists and doctors had their offices on the second floor, and the Gem Pharmacy was downstairs. Any prescriptions written by doctors in the building could be filled in the same place; it continued operating as a pharmacy until about 1971. Ninth Street was the center of the black business community in Little Rock.

The street was a city within a city. African Americans lived and worked in what was known as the Ninth Street corridor. "Little Harlem" was the informal name of this community, and it was a busy little area. White-operated businesses were primarily on Main Street, to the east.

Confectioners whose homemade goodies "were to die for," pharmacies, grocery stores, jewelers and hotels each had their own storefronts. Taxi companies, mortuaries and theaters were part of the scene as well. The barber and beauty shops were the most populated locations because they were the source of the latest gossip.

Service stations and restaurants were also some of the businesses located on the "line," a reference made to the area and in particular the street itself. Little Rock's "line" was right up there with Atlanta's Hunter Street and Tulsa's Greenwood Avenue.

A researcher gathering information about the history of the area interviewed people who related stories about the exciting times in the neighborhood. The Dreamland Ballroom was where people could dance the night away while having fun with friends. It was well known for being part of the "Chitlin' Circuit," the collective name given to a string of African American performance venues throughout the eastern and southern United States.

It was a safe and acceptable place for African American musicians, comedians and other entertainers to perform during the age of racial segregation in the United States. Notable performers who got their start on the Chitlin' Circuit included Count Basie, Cab Calloway, Duke Ellington, Ella Fitzgerald, Sammy Davis Jr., Redd Foxx and many more.

In an era of segregation, life on Ninth Street provided a sense of community to the African American people in the area. However, urban renewal was coming, and desegregation was on the horizon, as well as construction of Interstate 630, an east-west freeway that was to join downtown Little Rock to the western side of the city. Over time, the community moved away, and Ninth Street became a shell of its former self. But now there's hope for the return of the Dreamland Ballroom.

There were three buildings left standing in 1982, and one was Taborian Hall. It was listed on the National Register of Historic Places during that year. To quote from the book *Sentinels of History*, "Taborian Hall remains intact today largely through the efforts of the late Dr. Ruth Patterson, representing the Association for the Study of African-American Life and History, and Mike Shinn, a historian with Arkansas Historic Preservation Program." It also remains intact because of Kerry McCoy.

From the moment Ms. McCoy first walked into the ballroom, she glanced around the room and saw extravagant pink light fixtures surrounding the colossal stage, large box seats projecting over what appeared to be the dance floor and a balcony at the opposite end of the room facing the stage. Faded salmon pink walls, exposed bricks and trim with diamond shapes were scattered throughout the room.

She stood there staring as she tried to envision how it must have looked back in the beginning—"simply magnificent," she thought. It was a room where elegance once flowed and the audience was entertained by the best in the black entertainment world. Her experience was overwhelming, and she knew she wanted this building as soon as possible.

As mentioned earlier, Ms. McCoy became the owner of the building in 1991—the place she once admired and dreamed about. Today she can be proud of her accomplishments. The ballroom is again being used for entertaining events, and the first floor is a showroom and gift shop where displays of patriotic flags, clothes and jewelry can be found.

But there's more to be found—and heard—in the building. And people other than the employees have experienced it.

Shortly after the ballroom opened in 2011, a musical group called the 101 Runners was scheduled to entertain a large group of people. Before the performance, the group took some time to tour the building, and they experienced a few surprises.

They were members of an African American/Native American tribe out of the New Orleans area. Several of the group's members said they could feel "a welcoming presence" in the entire building, specifically in the ballroom—a feeling that someone was saying, "Come in, come to our place, and enjoy yourselves."

Maybe the "swing music" heard by Flag and Banner employees is by musicians from days gone by? Perhaps, as spirits do, they have returned to a place that they liked in their lifetimes.

I stopped by one day with some out-of-town visitors, all women, and took them upstairs. One remarked about hearing some faint music that sounded "happy." She could also hear people talking in soft whispered voices. She told me about her experience as we left the building.

On one occasion, when the store was open on a Saturday, employees heard someone walking above them on the second floor. The showroom is open on the weekend but the offices are closed upstairs, yet the floor above was creaking as if people were walking around. The sounds were coming from multiple locations.

Taborian Hall has survived urban renewal, as well as the neglect it suffered through the years. It is a survivor in its own right. Now, as you drive down Ninth Street, there it stands, as regal as when it was first built. During the night, lights from the street spotlight the large American flag outside the front door. That sight alone will give you a chill.

Look up to the third-floor windows, and see if you can spot a ghost looking back at you. Perhaps you might even hear some music coming from the same location, just as others have.

CHAPTER 7
LITTLE ROCK CITY HALL

Anyone who works in a building after-hours knows how creepy and scary the place can be. The slightest noise can be distracting, and the mind begins to think about all sorts of things that could be responsible for the noise.

I enjoy talking with the people who work late at night in these buildings—the people who walk the halls and deal with the unknown sounds. They may be security guards or other types of night-shift employees, but no matter where they work or who they are, they have stories to tell.

Working in the Little Rock City Hall is just as eerie as any other old building, according to what I've been told. Our city government has been conducting business there since 1908, the year it opened. City leaders have their offices located there, as do several hundred city employees. Occasionally, someone says he or she has had a paranormal experience.

A few years ago, I was there on business and, just out of curiosity, asked an employee if she had ever worked late at night or heard anything unusual. Much to my surprise, she answered, "Yes." I asked for an explanation, and she told me her story:

> *I was working late one night and had said goodbye to my coworkers. I then locked myself in the office. You immediately become "aware" of your surroundings when you're alone and want to work as quickly as possible so you can leave. Quietness sets in and you can hear a pin drop as well as your heart beating. I heard footsteps faintly approaching in the hallway—my heart rate picked up a beat as the steps got closer.*

A current picture of Little Rock City Hall, minus the dome that was originally built on top of the building when constructed. *Photo by David Hoge.*

> *I was hoping it was security making rounds and checking on what was going on. I heard the door unlock and a friendly voice say, "Security, is anyone here?" I answered "yes" and we talked about things in general and how long I planned on staying. He left, and I continued my work. It wasn't long before I heard a door shut out in the hallway. I thought it was probably security, but then it happened again and this time it sounded like someone was moving furniture across the floor. I thought, "What in the world is going on here?" I looked out in the hallway but didn't see anyone or hear any more noise. After that, I left!*

I asked if she thought the building had ghosts and she said, "Something was making all that noise and it wasn't human—so yes, I guess we do have ghosts." When I pass by city hall today, I think about her and wonder if she still works there. If she does, is it late at night?

Located at the corner of Broadway and Markham Street, you'll pass city hall just before you drive over the Broadway Bridge into North Little Rock. The original city hall was located on the upper floor of a liquor store a few blocks east of where it is today. The city was growing, and it became necessary to expand into more abundant accommodations.

In 1903, Little Rock elected a new mayor, W.E. Lenon, and by his second term in 1905, he could clearly see that the city needed to construct a city hall that would meet the city's administration needs for years to come. The small area that housed the workplace for Little Rock's city government was no longer able to handle the workload.

Charles Thompson, a local architect who was well known throughout the state, was chosen to work on the project. He had already gained fame from the many architecturally diversified structures he had designed. Thompson was one of the top, if not the top, architects in the state.

Five aldermen were appointed in February 1906 by Mayor Lenon to supervise the planning of the building. Several months later the plans were revealed but were met with opposition because they included an auditorium. The idea of adding a wing that would house a municipal auditorium was thought to be wasteful spending of the city's money.

The plans were disregarded, and Thompson went back to the drawing board and came up with a simpler design. The new plan was accepted in September 1906, and the estimated cost to build it was $175,000.

The construction was finished in two years, and an open house took place on April 15, 1908. The public was invited to visit their new city hall. Thompson designed the building in the Italian Renaissance Revival style.

Employees had begun moving into their offices a month before the official opening and were proud to work in their new quarters. The citizens were just as excited because Little Rock was growing into a metropolis, and the brand-new city hall looked distinguished in its position on the river's edge. It was a significant sign that Little Rock was growing.

In 1927, a local woman, Bernie Babcock, founded the Museum of Natural History and Antiquities. I mentioned in an earlier chapter that she was a distant aunt of mine. Mrs. Babcock began soliciting museum pieces and artifacts from all around the country. This was in response to criticism from H.L. Mencken, who said Arkansans were "bumpkins" who lacked cultural centers. Mencken was an American journalist, magazine editor and critic who wrote negatively about the South and Arkansas.

Mrs. Babcock was a distinguished author and the first Arkansas woman to be included in the *Authors and Writers Who's Who*. She published more than forty novels, and numerous tracts and newspaper and magazine articles. In addition, she was an authority on young Abraham Lincoln.

The antiquities arrived in Little Rock by rail. Little Rock now had a fine museum that was comparable to any other in the country. The initial location was a storefront on Main Street, where she had several sensational exhibits that included taxidermy specimens.

By 1929, Mrs. Babcock's museum needed more room and financial support. She was given permission to occupy the third floor of city hall. It was unfinished, but the room was sufficient for her needs. She bargained with electricians and carpenters to put in the needed equipment. Because the room was unheated, she wore her fur coat to work during the winter months.

The cherished pieces were packed and transported to their new home at city hall. The museum remained in this location for more than fifty years before relocating to the Tower Building at the Little Rock Arsenal.

For many years, her portrait was displayed in the hallway of city hall, a public gesture to give thanks and appreciation for her hard work. The portrait accompanied her museum pieces to the Tower Building and later the Museum of Discovery.

Today, many of Babcock's antiquities are housed in other museums throughout the country. The museum's presence in city hall contributed to the building's lengthy history.

A unique feature of the original city hall doesn't exist anymore: the dome on top of the roof. It was situated on a platform and rose above the treetops. This landmark could be seen in all directions for miles around. After fifty years of being exposed to the elements, it was in need of repair. The damage to the dome was described as "severe." The wooden supports and copper cladding—a metal sheath that was attached to the metal dome—were in bad shape.

At the time, Pratt Remmel was the mayor, and he budgeted money to have the dome repaired. However, all plans for renovation were abandoned when Remmel lost reelection to a third term in 1955 to Woodrow Mann. Mayor Mann made the decision not to repair the dome and conducted an informal public inquiry that listed three items for consideration.

The choices were: repair the dome, replace the dome with an aluminum one or remove it. Anyone could vote on this matter; being a resident of Little Rock was not a necessary requirement. The results revealed that the public wanted the dome removed—the vote was by a slim margin, however. The

An early postcard picture of Little Rock City Hall when the original dome was atop the building. Years later, it had to be removed due to destruction by the elements. *Postcard courtesy of the Karcher Candy Company.*

dome was taken apart piece by piece and removed, and any thoughts of replacing it were never given a second thought. The consensus was to spend city money on necessary expenses.

It wasn't until 1960 that improvements were made on the aging structure of city hall itself. Air-conditioning was installed, and the numerous windows that enabled natural light and fresh air to come in were bricked up, an effort to be more energy-efficient. Up until then, there was always a cross-current of air flowing through the building when the windows were opened—sealed shut, it must have felt somewhat claustrophobic to the employees who were used to being able to open the windows.

Little Rock's population was growing and moving westward. New homes were built in neighborhoods that sprang up; the suburbia movement was in full force. Many jobs moved west, too. Shopping centers opened in these neighborhoods, and a number of stores in the traditional downtown area closed. The outskirts were becoming the center of town, rather than the downtown area continuing to be the center of commerce.

Because Little Rock's citizens were leaving the downtown area, serious consideration was given to constructing another city hall farther west, to make the center of city government easier for the public to access. Talk of relocating continued into the 1970s and early 1980s, although some renovation had been taking place. The police and fire departments had moved out of city hall into new facilities, and their vacated spaces became rooms for storage.

By 1984, the decision was made to stay at the existing location. Renovation plans were drawn and construction began with hope that the restoration would bring people back downtown. Some other buildings in the downtown area had become vacant and were boarded up.

By 1988, the newly renovated and restored city hall opened its doors, and those walking through the threshold felt they were walking back into time. The interior had been restored to its 1908 appearance, and those bricked-up windows that had blocked the light for so long were now opened and sunshine could now filter into the once-sheltered offices.

One of the renovated areas was made into a workout room for employees, and it is in this area that employees have experienced an unusual occurrence. Could it possibly be paranormal in some way? There is no other explanation for what was witnessed. As told to me by a city employee, it appears that on occasion, the sounds of someone using equipment in an adjoining room can be heard.

Upon checking it out, the employees discover that no one is present—yet it was perfectly clear that what they heard was the workout equipment being used. Do you think ghosts exercise in the afterlife?

For the past forty years, a movement has been underway to encourage people to move back downtown. Little Rock's fine old homes with different architectural styles are being purchased and restored to their original state. Old buildings that once housed thriving businesses that eventually closed are now becoming part of this new downtown growth.

Historic preservation organizations and societies are becoming involved in Little Rock's preservation efforts. These groups are helping interested parties acquire information about what is needed for authenticity for preservation purposes.

Little Rock's leaders felt that the old buildings along Markham Street, east of Main Street, should be restored. They were vital during Little Rock's river port days. This idea led to the birth of the River Market, a retail, restaurant and residential area.

The buildings in the River Market area had been vacant for years, and restoration would take time. An architectural term, "adaptive reuse," is a significant way to describe what took place. For instance, a brick building that was once home to a furnace company is now the Clinton Museum Store. The triangular building housing the Cox Creative Center was once the Cox Machinery Company.

Most of the older buildings in this area have been restored and are now the locations of restaurants, gift shops, museums and residences. A multi-use amphitheater was built on the river's edge for outdoor concerts and church services.

New hotels, condos and apartment buildings have been added to the River Market area. The changes downtown have encouraged some people to consider moving there. The mixture of our town's history with modern-day influence makes this area one of Little Rock's top attractions.

On April 15, 2008, a public announcement headline read, "Little Rock City Hall Celebrates Century of Service." The article stated:

> *Surrounded by over 200 well-wishers, Little Rock's 71st and 72nd mayors blew out candles on a birthday cake to celebrate the 100th birthday of Little Rock City Hall. Current Mayor Mark Stodola and former Mayor Jim Dailey were joined by local and state elected officials, City Manager Bruce T. Moore and other City staff, and Little Rock citizens at the birthday party.*
>
> *"We wanted to take the time to commemorate this occasion and to celebrate 100 years of service to the citizens of Little Rock," said City Manager Moore.*

City hall has remained the center of Little Rock government from the onset, while other nearby buildings have been used for a variety of businesses and government offices.

If city hall had been relocated years ago, I feel that we would not have the movement of people coming back downtown. Since 1908, it has been standing tall even though changes took place over its more than one hundred years. By the end of the next one hundred years, it may still be standing proud. One thing is certain; the ghosts who haunt the building have never left, and they exercise on top of that!

CHAPTER 8

ROBINSON CENTER MUSIC HALL

The hour was late and a security guard was near the end of her shift. She was in the basement of one of Little Rock's well-known buildings, Robinson Center Music Hall, a place where Broadway shows are staged and concerts and ballet recitals are performed. She was making rounds a few levels down from the stage area and was looking forward to her shift change.

The guard was in the exhibition hall "bullpen," as it is commonly referred to by employees of Robinson Center. The hall was set up for an event to be held the next day. The hall is the center's locale for large groups that require ample square footage for their events.

There wasn't much light, and security personnel always carry a flashlight just in case they need one. The shift was about to change in fifteen minutes, and our security guard was beginning her last round. Just as she was getting started, she heard what sounded like running water. The sound quickly changed to that of rushing water.

Now she really became concerned and thought the water might burst through the closed doors into the hall. Using her flashlight, she checked around the door facing to see if water was trickling through the cracks—no sign yet.

She waited and watched, anticipating that the water was about to burst through the doors. She looked at the setup for the next day's show and thought how terrible it would be for the water to flood the area. What could she do, she asked herself? She started to sit down while thinking about the situation—and the sound stopped. She stood up—and it started again. How strange and surreal, she thought. What's causing this?

About that time, the doors opened and her relief, the next shift's security guard, walked in—without a sign of water anywhere! The guards exchanged greetings, and the puzzled guard left. Later, when her supervisor asked how her shift went, she mentioned hearing water.

"Oh, you heard it too," responded the supervisor.

"Why, yes, have you?" the guard inquired.

"Yes, I actually followed the sound to a closet and upon opening the door, it stopped," her supervisor said. The guards didn't know what caused these sounds or where they could find an answer.

I'm an intense listener when someone is telling me a story about an "unusual occurrence," and this tale held a special interest for me when the security guard related it to me. It didn't seem to be the usual paranormal type of activity, yet it was unexplainable. When you are in the hall by yourself, it's easy to think the place is scary.

To my knowledge, Robinson Center's water sound has never been explained, so it remains an unsolved mystery. The building is high up on the bank of the Arkansas River, and the sound could possibly be related to past floods that struck the area years ago—some type of residual haunting.

The following is a definition from Dave Juliano's website, *The Shadowlands: Ghosts and Hauntings*:

> *A residual haunting is a playback of a past event. The apparitions involved are not spirits; they are "recordings" of the event. I believe that this will be the first type of haunting that mainstream researchers will recognize and study. There are numerous theories on how these residual hauntings come to be.*

Robinson Center Music Hall was built as a project under the Public Works Administration, a part of President Franklin Roosevelt's New Deal. Our country was going through the Great Depression, and Roosevelt's New Deal was a group of programs designed to get the country back on its economic feet.

Roosevelt's plan was formulated during his first term and focused on what historians call the "3Rs": relief, recovery and reform. This government program was working toward "relieving" the unemployed and poor by putting them to work, "recovery" of the economy to normal levels and "reform" of the financial system to prevent a repeat depression.

Joseph Taylor Robinson was a prominent statesman from Little Rock. He supported Roosevelt's New Deal and was the U.S. senator from Arkansas during this time. He had previously served one term in the Arkansas House of Representatives, a decade as a U.S. representative in Washington and a few months as governor.

In 1913, he moved from the governor's office to the U.S. Senate, during which time he became the Senate majority leader. In 1928, he was a candidate for vice president of the United States and was a running mate to presidential candidate Alfred E. Smith. However, Herbert Hoover, who preceded Roosevelt, won the election by a landslide.

Robinson was a powerful man, and Roosevelt liked him. In fact, when Roosevelt came to Little Rock for a visit, he stayed at the senator's home.

Robinson was instrumental in acquiring major projects for Arkansas, and one of those was a much-needed civic auditorium in Little Rock. Up until that point, the only place that had the capacity to handle large public events was the auditorium at Little Rock High School, later renamed Little Rock Central High School.

A requirement of Public Works Administration funding was the stipulation that local money be used to supplement the federal funding for a project. So on January 26, 1937, Little Rock voters approved a bond referendum to provide the funds for the auditorium and other projects. Some of the money was divided and given to the public library for the construction of additions. The African American community wanted a city park, so the other portion of the money was used for that.

The architects selected for the new auditorium were George Wittenberg, Lawson Delony and Eugene Stern. They had an outstanding reputation for the work they had done in designing some of the most impressive buildings in Little Rock, as well as the rest of the state. (Just a side note—Mr. Delony was a family friend and suggested that a broom closet be added to the blueprints of my parents' home when it was under construction in 1959.)

On December 27, 1937, the groundbreaking for the new auditorium took place and construction began on what would become one of Little Rock's distinctive buildings.

The building was named in honor of Senator Robinson because of his hard work in making this dream come true, but, on a sad note, he never had a chance to appreciate this honor because he died in 1937, several months before construction began.

The construction of the Robinson Center Music Hall took two years, and it was finished on December 8, 1939. The city of Little Rock officially took ownership of the building in the later part of January 1940. A few weeks later in February, a formal dedication took place. Initially called the Joseph Taylor Robinson Memorial Auditorium, the building's name was changed

A postcard view of the newly constructed Joseph Taylor Robinson Memorial Auditorium. It was built in the mid-1930s to honor one of Little Rock's notable citizens, who unfortunately died before seeing it. *Postcard courtesy of the Karcher Candy Company.*

in 1973 to the Robinson Center Music Hall. Today, people refer to it simply as the Robinson Center.

The original proposed cost of the project was $655,000, but the actual amount spent was $855,000, $200,000 over the established budget. It's located across the street from Little Rock City Hall and the Pulaski County Courthouse. This intersection is quite impressive with its stately buildings.

A feature of the auditorium is the quality of sound, whether the voices of actors or music from a symphony. This great achievement is the result of careful planning from the beginning and the technology of the time.

The ceilings and walls in the main auditorium area were built with acoustical board set in panels between the pyramid columns. This setup enables the room to have near-perfect sound and suggests that the planners were interested in using advanced theater technology in their design.

The main auditorium includes the stage, arena, mezzanine, dressing rooms and balcony seating. The other part of the building houses lecture and exhibit halls, as well as meeting rooms. The exhibition hall is where the aforementioned security guard heard the sound of running water near the doors and closet.

At the time of construction, it was impossible to imagine the multiple uses this grandiose building could provide. A basketball court was set up in the auditorium, and local high school games were among the first events that took place after it opened. Musical concerts, ballet and on-the-road shows were a few more types of public entertainment that used the auditorium as a venue.

According to *The Encyclopedia of Arkansas History and Culture*, there were many world-famous performers and speakers who appeared on stage. Louis Armstrong, Ella Fitzgerald, Duke Ellington and Ray Charles were a few of the African American entertainers who performed here in the midst of desegregation that was taking place in the Little Rock school system.

During the 1940s and 1950s, seating was often segregated by race. A local white citizen who was a music manager and promoter tried to reverse this policy. His actions led to his arrest in the 1960s when he tried to sit with the black audience. Some concerts were canceled because of the segregated seating.

Other prominent entertainers, celebrities and political figures came to Little Rock. Katharine Hepburn, Mae West, Gene Autry, Bob Hope, Ethel Barrymore, Guy Lombardo, Eleanor Roosevelt and Dwight D. Eisenhower were some of the headliners.

The Arkansas Symphony Orchestra considers Robinson Center Music Hall its home and has performed there since 1966. The auditorium underwent extensive renovation in 1973 with underground parking added in the place of a lower performance hall.

With seats numbering 2,609, the auditorium can accommodate a large crowd. Added to the National Register of Historic Places on February 21, 2007, it stands among neighboring buildings on Markham Street that are also on the register.

Built in the Art Deco architectural style, it will never have an outdated appearance. I enjoy watching the groups of schoolchildren who come from all over the state to visit our city. They may be in town to see an attraction at the Robinson Center. Their yellow school buses are parked throughout the city while the children take in a ballet, musical concert or Broadway show. As they watch the activity on stage, they may be unaware of the man named Robinson who secured the money to build this dynamic structure. Children now have an opportunity to experience an event they may not otherwise have been able to see. It's quite an adventure to come to the capital city and be exposed to cultural attractions that will enhance their education.

Another attraction of sorts, or perhaps better defined as an incident, is present throughout the building. It's not publicly known and appears to especially exist on the lower levels where the exhibition hall is located. Could

Joseph Taylor Robinson Memorial Auditorium is known today as the Robinson Center Music Hall. It's home to the Arkansas Symphony and hosts other entertainment, such as Broadway shows. *Photo by David Hoge.*

it be a paranormal occurrence or just an example of a vivid imagination? When several people experience something out of the ordinary and it's unexplainable, we suspect paranormal activity. The untraceable source of running water that's been heard by several people late at night is an example.

In recent times, I talked with some people who work at Robinson Center about the odd things they've experienced. The old timers tell a story that's been around for years. A man named Henry worked on the construction site but had an accident and died. Since that time, people have heard unexplained sounds or had other sensations. For example, they hear what sounds like someone walking across the stage, doors shutting or objects sliding across the floor. People sense cold areas, smell tobacco smoke and see the cloth batting moving above the stage as though a gentle breeze has entered the building.

The hallway under the stage, where the dressing rooms are located, is another area described as eerie. People have had the feeling that someone is down there with them, and they sometimes spot a shadowy figure at the end of the hallway. These occurrences are especially noticeable when alone.

For some reason, employees suspect that the spirit of Senator Robinson is present and is the one causing things to happen. They refer to the spirit as "J.T." The following excerpt from Wikipedia describes the day Robinson was found dead in his apartment and the subsequent reaction of the nation:

> *On July 14, just as the legislation seemed likely to split his party into two warring factions, Robinson's housekeeper found his pajama-clad body lying face down on his apartment floor. He had not given up the battle, but his heart had. Two days after Robinson's sudden death, stunned colleagues, friends, and family attended his funeral in the Senate chamber. His casket, blanketed with flowers, rested in the green-carpeted pit, the site of his greatest speeches. The Senate chaplain gave a brief sermon, and the Capitol Police escorted his body to a funeral train headed to Little Rock. Thousands of mourners traveled to the Arkansas Capitol to witness Robinson's lying-in-state ceremony and to express their grief and their enormous admiration for the majority leader: the "fightingest" man in the U.S. Senate.*

The building has a reputation of being haunted, no doubt about it, but the question remains, who is there? Do you think the spirit could be J.T. or Henry? Of course, the senator died before finishing his work in the Senate and had a strong "fighting" human spirit, but Henry died before finishing his work constructing the building. Perhaps they both exist. Imagine the statesman and the carpenter together—what a unique blend of spirits!

CHAPTER 9

ARGENTA HISTORIC DISTRICT

The Argenta Historic District is located in the downtown community of North Little Rock. Over the past several years, it has been transformed into a classy art district with a distinguished character.

Years ago, city leaders developed a long-range plan for renovating old buildings on Main Street. Some of them date back to the 1800s, when the area was called Argenta.

Today, most of the renovation is complete, and tenants of these grand old buildings are owners of restaurants, shops, a community theater and art galleries that feature local artists. A sign of the revival and culture of downtown North Little Rock is the Third Friday Art Walk, a public event that takes place on the third Friday of every month.

Within the walls of some of these old buildings, you will find resident ghosts. Some of the living human tenants are willing to talk about their "ghostly roommates" and share their experiences, while others would prefer not to talk about them.

TraX, a private club, is in a building that is believed to be haunted. The staff is aware of what appears to be two ghosts in this establishment. As with any haunting, one has to ask why a ghost would linger and not cross over to the other side—a common term used when referring to death. Later in this chapter, we'll learn more about those strange sightings. But first, let's learn a little about the history of North Little Rock.

If you look as far back as the nineteenth century, you will find that the name for the north shore was always changing. The leader of the community

The Argenta Historic District of North Little Rock was once the scene of railroad tracks running throughout the area, but today it is an upscale art district with galleries and various restaurants. *Photo by David Hoge.*

usually establishes town names, and because early North Little Rock had many leaders, the town went through frequent name changes.

According to the North Little Rock History Commission, Huntersville was the name most referred to when speaking of this area in the 1820s. The origin of this name has been in dispute among historians, but earlier writers claim that a ferry crossing the river from the Point of Rocks (the little rock) went to the "Huntersville Landing" on the opposite side of the river.

Richard DeCantillon Collins surveyed a one-hundred-acre tract in the area, and the settlement was named for him around 1840. It was always subject to flooding because of its geographic location to the Arkansas River. Farming was good because of deposits of silt from the flooding conditions, but hopes of founding a settlement became dismal.

Towns could be washed away in seconds by water rising from the river, and such was the case of DeCantillon. Without warning, the town was swept away in the flood of 1840, and anyone near this location would have been swept away also. Today, the remnants of the original tract lie between the Broadway and Main Street bridges and are protected by flood control structures on the Arkansas River.

The name Argenta has an interesting background. Thomas W. Newton Sr. was a local politician and president of a company that worked the Kellogg silver mine located about ten miles north of the river. In 1866, his family surveyed and platted a town site they called Argenta in honor of their father. Because of the sentiment shown for this name, the historic district is called that today.

In the 1830s, the forced relocation of the Five Civilized Tribes of Native Americans took place across the country, and the various routes came across the state of Arkansas. Referred to as the Trail of Tears, it was a long, hard journey that was devastating to the Native Americans. *The Encyclopedia of Arkansas History and Culture* states that an estimated sixty thousand people came through Arkansas by foot, horse or boat.

One route brought them through what is now North Little Rock; it was a crossroads and campground for the Native Americans. Communicable diseases spread quickly among the travelers, and a large number died. One of the travelers was Chief John Ross of the Cherokee Nation, a man held in high esteem by all who knew him.

He made the journey by boat with his children and wife, Quatie. During the trip, Quatie gave her blanket to a sick child, but by doing this kind gesture, she became gravely ill herself. By the time the group reached this part of the state, she was suffering from pneumonia and eventually died.

When the Ross family docked, her body was taken off the boat and buried somewhere in this area. The actual burial site is a mystery; her remains have never been found. A stone marker bearing her English name, "Elizabeth," was discovered in an old cemetery in Little Rock known as the Peabody Cemetery, but there was no evidence that her body had been there.

All remains were exhumed from this location and interred in what was then a new cemetery in Little Rock, Mount Holly. The exhumations were necessary to make room for the construction of a federal building.

Although Quatie's remains were not found when the marker was unearthed, Albert Pike, a prominent attorney in Little Rock, requested that the marker be placed in his lot at Mount Holly. The marker was fragile, and years later was replaced with a replica donated by the Historic Arkansas Museum. The museum stores the original in its archives.

According to the *Mount Holly Cemetery Burial Index*, the group known as the United Daughters of 1812 placed an additional marker in Pike's lot. Quatie died February 1, 1839, and the inscription reads: "Cherokee Indian wife of John Ross, Indian Agent and Chief of Cherokee Tribe; died on board boat en route to Indian Territory (per 5 Feb 1839 *Arkansas Gazette*); her English name: Elizabeth Brown Hensley Ross."

Quatie has two markers side by side, one engraved with her English name and the other with her Native American name. People pay their respects by leaving tokens on both of her gravestones: coins, crystals and natural items are left on top of the markers. According to Native American legend; these trinkets will help her into the spirit world.

According to lore, some people believe they have seen Quatie's ghost. Perhaps she's on a quest to find the family that left her behind as they continued their journey to Oklahoma. Long after the Native Americans were gone, people were still coming and going in downtown North Little Rock.

By the turn of the twentieth century, railroads were populating the Argenta area. There was a network of rails running in different directions, and tracks diverting to the side were included in this maze. In fact, the modern-day business TraX is named for one of the sidetracks. It is a private club and home to a well-known ghost story, as mentioned earlier.

The building that houses TraX was the last one constructed on its block in 1920 and was unique because of its design. Originally, it housed two separate buildings with a basement under one roof but had a common wall with separate entrances. Soon after the building was completed, Miss Birdie, a madam, opened a brothel on one side.

Next door was a dark, dingy saloon with a dirt floor. What a convenience for the railroad workers who were interested in relaxing, having a few drinks and keeping company with a "woman of the evening." This arrangement was an accident waiting to happen; in fact, the area was considered so rough that it was off limits to the military. The railroad workers were competing with the riverboat workers for the attention of Miss Birdie's girls.

According to the legend, a patron (rumored to be a man named Maxwell) was visiting the bar before walking the path over to see his love in the brothel. Her name was Anastasia, and she was very attractive, young and devoted to Maxwell. While in the bar, he overheard some men talking about how they had "just seen" Anastasia, and he became jealous.

He immediately went over to the brothel to confront her with the allegations. She, of course, denied any wrongdoing, but in his anger, he took his knife and cut her from one ear to the other and then picked up her lifeless body and threw it from the balcony down to the alley below. Then he ran off. Years later, Maxwell returned, got into a fight with some rough men and was killed on the spot.

The brothel and bar were forced to close their doors, and the building was eventually sold to an undertaker. He used the basement to prepare remains for burial. Some say a tunnel was created so he could move the bodies to the funeral home across the street and go undetected from the public view. The mortuary eventually closed, and the undertaker left all of his embalming equipment in the basement.

Over the years, the building was bought and sold by different individuals who used it for different reasons. It had been a saloon, brothel, mortuary and later a coffeehouse by the name of Maxwell's.

Other stories tell of motorcyclists riding their bikes through the building after stopping at the bar for a drink. In 1991, Brian Bosworth, a former professional football player turned actor, rode his motorcycle along with some other bikers through the building's window. It was an action scene in the movie *Stone Cold* that he starred in.

A couple bought the place in 1996 and wanted to completely renovate it. The rough and tumble reputation it had endured in past years was about to change. The new owners were amazed to find that the beautiful tin ceiling and skylights were all original to the building. They wanted to offer a fine dining restaurant and be a part of the North Little Rock plan for improving the downtown area.

Dreams of linen-covered tables with crystal glassware, fine china, elegant silverware and the finest of furnishings were about to become a reality, a long way from the building's early days as a saloon and brothel. The restaurant opened as Diamond Jim's Fine Dining, and it was a beautiful place to eat.

Unfortunately, their dream didn't last long because of the continued restoration of downtown. Construction sites made it difficult to walk to the restaurant. It was an upscale place designed to create a fine dining experience, but walking across wooden planks with open trenches discouraged patrons. Eventually, the doors closed, and the building was vacant for several years.

The current occupants of the building operate the private club TraX and realized after leasing the building that it came with a ghost or two. They have posted on their website their personal experiences in dealing with supernatural occurrences.

It was during the time of their renovation of the building that they began to notice some very unusual things. For example, carpenters had a difficult time doing their work because the extension cords kept losing power. It certainly slowed down the progress of renovation, and there was never an explanation as to why this kept happening. This type of activity is a common occurrence with spirits; it's a way ghosts try to make themselves known, by "messing" with the tools. The staff also witnessed water running in the kitchen and bathrooms that no human had turned on.

The staff saw other suspected paranormal events, such as the oven turning itself on, lights flickering, the pilot lights on the stove turning on and off and things being moved around the building frequently. Other mysterious occurrences have involved the bar area. The top shelf behind the bar holds crystal stemware, and one night, the shelf mysteriously came out over the bar and dropped to the floor, smashing the crystal into thousands of pieces. The glass shelf did not break, and no one was near the bar at the time this happened.

The chef quit immediately after watching a breaker box door opening and closing for no apparent reason. Also, the computer system is kept in a secured area, and the staff discovered the computer turned on and letters and figures appearing on the monitor without explanation.

The owners have mentioned seeing a cloudy image of something that looks like a face in a mirror. People have seen doors opening without assistance and felt the soft touch of something brushing against their face or hair. They have felt cold spots at the foot of the stairs and had the sensation that someone was pushing an eating utensil out of their hands.

They believe that all of these experiences are the actions of their resident ghost and have named him Maxwell. He has been sighted twice, and the image of someone else is beside him. They would like to think that the other image is the ghost of Anastasia.

The owner has decided to keep a log on the ghostly activity and here is one of his entries:

> *Thursday, September 17, 2009*
> *I walked into the building today and every door bell* [sic] *was ringing. (We have three door bells.) I thought that maybe someone was playing a prank by taping the door bell button down but that was not the case. The only way that I could get the bells to stop ringing was to pull the batteries from them. Oh by the way, these were new batteries in the door bells so that could not have been the problem.—Philip*

Ghost stories are also told at other buildings in Argenta. Across the street and down a block from TraX is the Owens Funeral Building. The funeral home shut down years ago, but the building was renovated and several individual businesses are located there.

A story is told of a woman wearing black mourning clothes from head to toe. She also wears a black hat and has been seen walking the halls. When

The Owens Funeral Home is now the location of offices for a variety of businesses. *Photo by David Hoge.*

approached, she asks if this is where the funerals are located, then disappears around the corner.

Next door is a branch of the Laman Library, but it was once the location for city offices, including a fire station. Since becoming a branch library, the staff has noticed items being moved around or relocated and doors open that had been shut the night before or vice versa.

The Argenta Historic District is certainly an interesting place to visit. The curbs are lined with beautiful flowers, the buildings are renovated and active with a variety of businesses and people are encouraged to move downtown. Every year around Halloween, this area hosts the Anastasia Ball in honor of the young girl whose life ended violently and probably in vain.

It is believed by some that ghosts linger in a place when their death was traumatic and sudden. Whether you stroll along the three-block area or ride the vintage trolley, if you gaze into the buildings, you might catch a glimpse of Quatie, Maxwell and Anastasia or perhaps some other ghost.

Stroll along the river's edge and feel the chill that overtakes you while remembering you're walking where thousands of Native Americans were forcibly marched on their way to a new home. Many died here during this historic journey in our country's history. Perhaps now you will understand why ghosts linger and don't cross over to the other side.

CHAPTER 10
BAKER HOUSE BED AND BREAKFAST

Nestled between large trees and a private garden in the Argenta Historic District of North Little Rock is the Baker House Bed and Breakfast. The house has been described as an exceptional Queen Anne Victorian structure—one of the best examples in Arkansas of that type of ornate architecture. Artemus Colburn built the house at the corner of Monroe and Main Streets from 1896 to 1897. The street name was later changed from Monroe to Fifth.

Stories have been told about hauntings that take place there. For instance, during a few outdoor weddings in the private garden, a woman has appeared in the second-floor window. Although the wedding party knew that no one was in the house at the time, those that saw her would swear she was alive and real. She has appeared several times and has been photographed in the window. There are other accounts of hauntings and paranormal investigations that have taken place, but let's take a look into the history of the house first before we begin our journey into the spirit world.

Artemus Colburn was a watchmaker who was born in New Hampshire but eventually found his way to Arkansas. During the time he lived in the house, he and his wife raised three daughters. They opened their home to boarders, who were mostly railroad men, which made sense because North Little Rock, then named Argenta, was a railroad boomtown at the time.

After four years of living there, Colburn sold the house to George Davidson. In addition to selling the house, Colburn also liquidated other holdings and was rumored to be headed to Alaska in search of gold. It is

The beautiful country garden on the premises of the Baker House Bed and Breakfast is a prime location for weddings and other formal gatherings. *Photo by David Hoge.*

not known what happened to him after that, although according to the 1910 U.S. Census, he was living in Seattle, Washington.

George Davidson may have had his name on the deed of the house, but there are conflicting stories about whether he actually lived there. According to a *North Little Rock Times* article dated March 25, 1982, Davidson's daughter, Marguerite, is quoted as saying that her father was a mechanic for Missouri Pacific Railroad and bought the house from Colburn in 1901.

However, census records listed the Davidson family residing elsewhere during this time. Those records are contradicted by a notation that appeared in the *Times* announcing that Davidson had moved into the large brick residence at Fifth and Main. Regardless of whether or not he and his family lived there, George Davidson is shown to be the second owner of the house until 1916, when it was sold to Cadmus J. and Annie Baker.

Baker was the North Little Rock school superintendent from 1904 to 1906, and he operated a pawn broker business with his wife until 1939. The house remained in his family until the late 1900s, when Dr. Hampton Roy bought it in 1977. Roy sold the house in 2005. Despite the house changing hands, it still is referred to as the Baker House today.

When Roy owned the house, he applied to list it with the National Register of Historic Places, and the house was awarded that distinction in 1978. In the process, Roy learned of an interesting story about confusion over who built the house.

The legend goes back to Colburn's days, when the house was constructed. Historians thought that he was a native of North Little Rock and had become quite well known in England as a jockey. As the story goes, he was discouraged from living in his newly constructed house because he was black. However, this is far from the truth. Colburn and his wife were white, and he was a jeweler and watchmaker. He faced no obstacles to keep him from living in his house.

As far as I know, there has never been an explanation for why people confuse Colburn with Alonzo Clayton, a young black man who rose to fame as a jockey. He lived in Argenta during the late 1800s and was called by his nickname, Lonnie. Clayton became one of the highest-paid riders on the East Coast circuit during this time. In fact, on April 14, 2011, a historical marker was placed at the former location of Bashford Manor Farm in honor of Clayton and his success. His horse Azra was born at the farm located in Louisville, Kentucky.

Also, on that date, a local Louisville television station, WHAS11, quoted John Asher, a Churchill Downs spokesman, as he paid honor to Clayton. "He holds a spot in Kentucky Derby and their racing history that will never be surpassed. He is the youngest rider to win the Kentucky Derby in its 136-year history of the race—he was just fifteen years old when he rode Azra in that race." Clayton won more than twenty-four stakes races and rode in four Kentucky Derby races.

With his winnings, he came back home and built a house that was considered to be a fine example of Queen Anne architecture. Today it is listed on the National Register of Historic Places—an honor received in 1990. Swiss immigrant Joseph Engelberger bought it in 1912 and the house bears his name today.

The city north of Little Rock underwent several name changes during this period. During the 1890s, when the Baker House and Engelberger House were built, the area was called Argenta. It was unincorporated at the time, so Little Rock made it the eighth ward of that city by annexing it.

In the early part of 1904, the north shore reannexed the land and formed a new local government under the name of North Little Rock. However, another change was in the works to return the name to Argenta. Those in power eventually decided it was time to permanently change back to North Little Rock and it has remained so since 1917. What a confusing part of North Little Rock's history!

Baker House, in all its glory, stands alone among the office buildings that are its neighbors. A few cottage-style dwellings are located nearby, but Baker House is noticeably different. As one strolls down Main Street, you may be

The Baker House Bed and Breakfast is located in the heart of the Argenta Historic District. It's a fine example of Queen Anne Victorian architecture and has been completely restored. The suites are named for notable citizens in North Little Rock's history. *Photo by David Hoge.*

distracted by the vintage trolley traveling down the tracks in the street and by the restaurants, art galleries and sport bars. Then you come to Fifth Street and are mesmerized as you look toward the house.

I think some people, when they view a Queen Anne structure with towers and turrets, are reminded of photos they have seen of haunted houses. When my haunted tour groups unload in front of the house, they always want to go to the property's iron gate and look the place over. The entrance porch is inviting. Decorated with wooden spindles, spools and a "moon gate" entrance, it is attractive and makes a beautiful setting. A round tower is centered in front of the house and is three stories tall with a gabled roof. The wooden floor of the porch was replaced with concrete in the 1920s. The interior woodwork takes hold of your attention when you first enter the house. "Curley" pine is everywhere, and it's a pattern not often seen. Oak is another wood used in the fireplace mantels on the first floor.

The current owners bought it in 2005 and worked hard to update the landscaping and provide new furnishings. After two years, it opened as a bed-and-breakfast.

Each bedroom suite is named for a prominent city leader, such as Faucette, Matthews, Laman, Hays and Burns; all made a name for themselves in the community and were vital to the history of the town. Every suite has a private bath, which is a convenience for guests. The furniture, fabric, wallpaper and paint are typical of the Victorian period. Some suites have fireplaces and footed tubs. The owners have worked hard to make their guests feel at home and perhaps experience a trip back into time.

Instead of grabbing a health bar and a cup of coffee as you might do while dashing off to work or school, you are treated to a sit-down breakfast served on period china in the formal dining room. A restful night and delicious breakfast in a relaxing atmosphere is something to dream about.

There is another side to the Baker House B&B. As mentioned earlier, it is known to be haunted. Several guests have had some unusual experiences, and paranormal groups have been in the house to investigate.

One team was in the house by themselves and had an experience that scared them enough to make their hearts race rapidly. While setting up their equipment in one of the upstairs rooms, they could hear movement inside the house. One member was close to a locked door when suddenly, loud banging commenced—out of nowhere and without warning. Loud banging is a common paranormal occurrence there.

Another group experienced cold spots, the sensation of the touch of a hand and a tingle as they explored the rooms in the house. During an investigation, the investigator will ask if a "spirit" is present and if so, to say something or demonstrate somehow that they are present. Sometimes they will get a reaction from the spirit as mentioned above. Lucky ones may be able to hear a soft whispering voice.

According to the owners, children's voices have been recorded, along with an adult identifying himself as "Mr. Jefferson." The voices have been heard by guests as well. One of the owners sees shadowed images moving about the house. Could "Mr. Jefferson" be the construction worker who hanged himself from the rafters during a renovation project? He just might be the resident spirit, since his death was a traumatic one.

As mentioned earlier, the Baker House is one of the sites on our local haunted tour. The group disembarks across the street at a small park with sculptured pieces. It's an inviting peaceful place with the sound of water trickling in the fountain—a great place for a photo shoot. Just as the group is getting settled, we begin our walk toward Main Street and stop in front of the house to take pictures and see what may happen.

Late at night, the house takes on a different appearance than during the day. Most places do look different at night, but this spot is the exception and warrants a pause from our walk. As the story is told of its history and the woman who appears in the window during a garden wedding, all eyes are fixed and cameras are rolling. I think it's the Victorian architecture that creates the illusion of a haunted place. Its gabled roof, towers and turrets with lots of nooks and crannies add to the imagination.

I received an email one day from a woman who had been on our tour the night before. She was informing me that she and her daughter spent the night at the Baker House. They were influenced to do so after taking the tour and hearing about its history.

This is what she told me:

> *My daughter could not sleep as there was banging & knocking all night, our other breakfast companions at the Baker House heard this too before learning of our previous night's outing. I heard nothing but upon waking that next morning around 5, my usual time, the doorknob suddenly fell off while I was in the bathroom. I just laughed & told the spirit they had to do better than that as I knew not to pull the knob or I'd been in there until I woke the rest of the guests, lol.*

The house is surrounded by other haunted locations. Several are described in this book, but one story that has been told and written about for years should be mentioned. Across the street is the location of what was once the old jail, in a building that faces Main Street. In the 1930s, a racial incident took place when a prisoner was taken from jail by a mob and lynched. His spirit has been seen in the area, according to the legend.

The Argenta Historic District is full of history, both old and haunting. This is what draws people back to the area to live and work. North Little Rock started out as a railroad community and remains so today. It is an integral part of the Union Pacific Railroad system and proud of it. The citizens are friendly and offer true Southern hospitality.

The area is a great place to visit, and the Baker House would be the ideal location to spend the night. It's close to the trolley line, and there are various places to eat, art galleries to visit or a nice area for a casual walk. This small community draws crowds because of the various attractions nearby. They make you feel welcomed and at home with a small-town flair, and spending a night or two inside the Baker House would make your visit complete.

The reviews of the Baker House mention the comfort of the beds, the "outstanding breakfast" and the hospitable innkeeper and owners. The owners' website says the house offers "a delightful mixture of Southern hospitality and Victorian elegance." And, some believe, a ghost or two!

CHAPTER 11
JACKSONVILLE MUSEUM OF MILITARY HISTORY

Spirits haunt some of the most interesting places. We mortals don't know why they choose these locations, but we assume they must have a good reason. Some suspicious events have occurred at the Jacksonville Museum of Military History.

The land where the museum sits has been home to two structures. The first building, which no longer exists, was the administration office of an ordnance plant. There were six such plants built in the state during World War II, and Jacksonville was home to one of them.

The next structure was built on the same site and originally used as a funeral home. Today, the museum occupies that building. Whoever is actively haunting there is making themselves known to the employees of the museum. This area is rich in military history and haunts.

Occasionally the odor of cigarette smoke can be detected, but the staff assumes the smell is a remnant on some of the military artifacts on display. There are uniforms, firearms and personal items that military personnel carried while on active duty. Is it possible after sixty-plus years that a smoke odor would remain and be strong enough to be detected?

During World War II, the men of our nation were overseas fighting a war that would help us maintain our democratic government and way of life. The outcome would mean freedom for a large population of the world if the Allies won the war. So while this very important event in our world history took place, the women back home stepped up to the plate and worked in factories and on assembly lines. They left the security of their homes and took on the work normally done by men.

Ordnance plants sprang up around the country. Arkansas was centrally located and a prime location for the plants. Our business and political leaders rallied together to encourage the federal government to build them here in our state. Part of their argument was that the natural gas and coal resources were plentiful. Also, chances of enemy attack were slim because of the state's location in the middle of the United States. Arkansas' labor force was substantial.

The state leaders were convincing, and Arkansas became home to six ordnance plants that were located as far north as Pulaski County and as far south as the state lines of Louisiana and Texas. Their primary purpose, according to the website *The Encyclopedia of Arkansas History and Culture*, was to manufacture detonators, fuses, primers and bombs and establish proving grounds for testing munitions and rockets. Chemical agents that were needed in bombs and explosives were produced in these plants. Military staff supervised the operations of each plant, and they all relied heavily on civilian personnel.

Because able-bodied men were needed to fight on the front lines, the job of working in the ordnance plants fell to women and the disabled. Fourteen- and fifteen-year-olds lied about their ages in order to work. The need was great, and those left behind did what they could to help out. The nickname for women who worked in wartime factories was "Rosie the Riveter," a reference also made in a song written in 1942.

Jacksonville, in north Pulaski County, is located twenty minutes from Little Rock and, as already mentioned, was a location of one of the ordnance plants. It became a boomtown when the plant was built in 1941. With no housing available at first, the women lived in tents, their own automobiles or wherever they could find accommodations. Eventually, a two-hundred-unit trailer park was created and a housing project was built. Dormitories later opened on the plant site, as well as houses for key personnel.

On December 15, 1945, the administration building burned, and the cause could not be determined. The plant was closed by that time and production had ceased, but decontamination was still in progress. By 1946, other buildings that were part of the campus had to be moved or put up for sale. The layout of streets in Jacksonville has remained the same as when the ordnance plant was up and running. They cover several miles, and the circular drive in front of the museum is one of those original streets. It was in front of the administration building during the time the plant was active.

A few years after the fire, a structure resembling a two-story house was built by some individuals who offered funeral home services. The new building was constructed on top of the original foundation of the administration

The Jacksonville Museum of Military History is located at the former administration office for an ordnance plant. Hundreds of women worked at the plant during World War II while men were fighting overseas. The museum has numerous exhibits that honor the contributions made by local men, women, civilians and military, from the Civil War–era to present-day conflicts. *Photo by David Hoge.*

building. It remained a funeral home for many years until the owners decided to dissolve the business.

As was mentioned in the beginning of this chapter, the Jacksonville Museum of Military History occupies the building today. In May 2005, the museum opened its doors and has grown from a small museum with a few exhibits to an impressive institution. One of the first tasks was to hire a director, and DannaKay Duggar was selected. Ms. Duggar is an energized individual with a love of military history and is an asset to the success of the museum.

The goal of the supporters and Ms. Duggar was to provide information to the public through the exhibits. They have done this by emphasizing the important role of the military in this country as well as the Jacksonville area. Jacksonville also is home to Little Rock Air Force Base.

The museum is funded by private donations, grants and the Jacksonville Advertising and Promotions Commission. The museum offers exhibits on war and home front activities, dating from the Civil War, through the Cold War and up to ongoing military engagements, as well.

It was Ms. Duggar who shared her experience about the spirits that haunt the building. She and another staffer were closing up one night and heard a door slam shut in the distance. The building is quite large, and Ms. Duggar asked the employee if she had secured all of the doors in the back. The

The library, located inside the right wing of the Jacksonville Museum of Military History, was the site of a paranormal event. *Photo by David Hoge.*

response was yes. They went through the building rechecking doors and other areas but found no one, and nothing seemed out of the ordinary.

As stated earlier, cigarette smoke has been detected without the appearance of a cigarette. The employees suspect that it may be lingering odor from some of the World War II artifacts. Maybe what is lingering are the spirits of those whose possessions are in the museum!

A part of the building houses a library that is used for research and leisurely reading. On one occasion, a visitor was in the library and got hit by a book that flew out of nowhere. Another visitor to the building detected voices of unseen people and clearly heard the names of "Don" and "Dan." Interestingly, Don is the name of Ms. Duggar's brother, who is still alive, but her father, named Dan, is deceased.

Ms. Duggar welcomes all visitors, whether spiritual or human, with a warm, inviting smile. The doors are open from 9:00 a.m. to 5:00 p.m. Monday through Saturday.

The museum is located at 100 Veterans Circle in downtown Jacksonville. A visit is well worth the trip because of the unique and diversified exhibits—and, of course, it may be haunted.

CHAPTER 12
REED'S BRIDGE

Arkansas suffered greatly from the effects of the Civil War. While the area didn't experience the major battles that were so well known throughout other parts of the country, it did have its share of skirmishes. It was a horrific time, considering that citizens were expected to fight against a brother or friend—it all depended on where one lived.

Once the battle line was drawn, the enemy was on the "other" side, and it didn't matter what your relationship had previously been; they were now the opposing force. The politics of the nation and the reasons men went into battle were all as different as night and day, but this story is focused on a small skirmish that took place in Pulaski County and the history of the surrounding area.

Most of the battles in the Civil War were fought on Southern land, and even today artifacts are found that remind us of what took place over a century and a half ago. Visitors have discovered buttons, buckles, musket shot, jewelry and cannonballs.

It was estimated that more than 600,000 soldiers lost their lives during this four-year conflict, a staggering number compared with the fatalities from other wars our nation has fought.

This nation is peppered with ghost tours and stories about our haunted battlefields, including well-known sites such as Gettysburg, Antietam, Fredericksburg, Kennesaw Mountain National Battlefield and the Chickamauga National Military Park; even Valley Forge is haunted.

People who have witnessed unusual things in these places share the same experiences. Ghosts are seen roaming the battlefields, moaning mournfully as they search for their bodies; bushes make rustling sounds; people hear gunshots or cannon fire; voices are heard in the distance; and misty images appear.

Reed's Bridge is a twenty-minute drive north of Little Rock and is located in the city of Jacksonville. It is the site of a locally important Civil War battle that took place in August 1863 and is not immune to spirit adventures. Just like at other battlefields around the country, Reed's Bridge also has had some surreal events.

One day in recent years, a group of local people was doing landscape maintenance and decided to build a campfire. As they were working nearby, someone happened to glance over at the fire and noticed what appeared to be a body on the ground, with only the legs seen. The blaze obscured the view of the rest of the body.

The group's first thought was that someone had fallen and needed help. They dropped what they were doing to check it out. They were startled, to say the least, when, as they got closer to the fire, the legs disappeared and the body with it!

Thinking someone needed medical attention, another person tried to call for emergency assistance. Much to the surprise of the group, that person's cell phone did not work, although it had before the sighting. This experience left the group stunned, and they decided to leave. Of course, when they got back on the main road, the cell phone worked just fine.

(Some might say that cell phones act up occasionally because they are electronic. That's probably what happened here, but I don't think so. I had a surreal experience with my own phone. One morning during breakfast, it rang three times and each time the caller ID window displayed the cell phone's own number. After talking with a local wireless phone company representative, she said it was impossible for the phone to show its own number. She couldn't explain how it happened. Then I mentioned that, at that time, I worked in a haunted building and suggested that could be the problem. With that, she said, "Your phone is haunted, so take it back with you when you leave." So, I left the store with a new phone and the old one in my purse. After returning home, I put the "haunted" one in a dresser drawer for storage, but the alarm kept going off until I removed the battery.)

The history of Reed's Bridge begins with a family of a different name. According to *The Encyclopedia of Arkansas History & Culture*, a settler named Jacob Gray moved to Arkansas from Williamson County, Tennessee, in the early nineteenth century.

Gray and his brother Shared came to Arkansas in 1820 initially without their families and spent their first winter here. The following spring, the children of Jacob moved with their spouses and offspring to join their father and uncle in their new home state. With this brood, the area where they made their homestead became known as "Gray Settlement" and today is referred to as Gray Township.

Jacob Gray's eldest son, Samson, became the authority figure and head of the family, a role he would remain in for years to come. As a contractor, he oversaw the construction of portions of a road that was built from Memphis, Tennessee, to Little Rock. Part of the road building job included building a bridge over the Bayou Meto, a local stream that originates in Pulaski County.

Samson Gray eventually acquired a contract to carry U.S. mail with stops along the way. Soon a stagecoach route was added, and the mail and passenger services were combined. The Gray family home became a popular stagecoach stop, and their log home was a well-known "public house."

The routes of the Trail of Tears came through Arkansas in the 1830s. During the Indian Removal and Relocation Movement ordered by the federal government, several tribes from the eastern part of the United States traveled through Arkansas.

Some routes used portions of the Southwest Trail during their migration. Many lives were lost on the Trail of Tears. The Gray family provided rations to the Native Americans as they journeyed west in search of their new home in Oklahoma.

The Southwest Trail was used by settlers traveling from the St. Louis, Missouri, area. According to different sources, the trail was a collection of routes that ended in the Red River Valley of Texas. The trail crossed our state diagonally from the northeast corner, running through the center and exiting in the southwest corner. It avoided the swampland of the eastern part of the state and the mountains to the west. Many people who moved to Arkansas came via the trail. It would be known at one point as Military Road.

Another route, also called the military road, was the one whose construction was overseen by Samson Gray. The east-west military road, built first from Memphis to Little Rock and then to Oklahoma, intersected the Southwest Trail. You can still find the latter Military Road today in Jacksonville. It's also called Arkansas Highway 294. A remnant of the Gray Settlement is called Heritage Park, and it is located along this route. Visitors can view historic panels to learn about the history of the area. The western end of Highway 294 connects to Arkansas Highway 161, and this intersection is just north of where our story takes place.

When Samson Gray died, his brother Thomas carried on the responsibilities of managing the stagecoach stop and supplying rations to the Native Americans. According to *The Encyclopedia of Arkansas History & Culture*, Thomas filed a petition by July 1838 to build a toll bridge across Bayou Meto to replace the original bridge.

He sold the charter to John H. Reed in October of the same year, and Reed completed the bridge the following year. From this moment on, the bridge became known as Reed's Bridge.

For the next seven years, Reed worked the toll bridge until his death in 1845, and then the responsibility transferred to his widow and children. The Reeds saw all types of transportation crossing their bridge as each person paid a toll.

By 1858, a segment of the Butterfield Overland Mail Route was established along the road, and it continued to be a main thoroughfare. The bridge operated until it was burned on August 27, 1863, during the Civil War Battle of Reed's Bridge.

In that battle, Confederate troops were ordered to hold the Union soldiers marching toward Little Rock at bay for as long as possible. During the battle, they set fire to the bridge in an attempt to slow down the aggressive enemy.

The modern-day Reed's Bridge was built near the location of the original bridge. During the Civil War, it was burned by the Confederate army in an attempt to keep the Union army from advancing into Little Rock. *Photo by David Hoge.*

As Union troops made every effort to put out the flames, the Confederates opened fire, killing seven and wounding thirty-eight.

This action delayed the Union army from advancing, which was good for the Confederates; they numbered only 1,300 but held off 6,000 Union soldiers, according to members of the Civil War Round Table of Arkansas and Central Arkansas Civil War Heritage Trail Association, who prepared the *Little Rock Civil War Campaign* brochure.

The bridge was impassable because of the damage caused by the fire, and this created a temporary stalemate. However, a few days later, the Union army found a place to the south where they could ford the creek. They crossed Bayou Meto at Shallow Ford and marched into Little Rock, seizing the state capitol building on September 10, 1863.

Today the Reed's Bridge Historical Society owns some acreage within what was the 412-acre battlefield. Several years ago, research was done to assist the society in developing its members' ideas and prepare for the construction at the site. A multi-phase plan was developed, and today visitors can tour the grounds and immerse themselves in history. The group is attempting to make everything authentic from the ground up.

The *Civil War Buff* newsletter reported on a project conducted by a group of high school students who helped clear an acre of land where an 1860s replica homestead was built. The trees that were taken down were used to build the structures. What a great educational experience for the students and others who participated in this endeavor!

The homestead is located on the original battlefield. It includes a kitchen, barn and other cabins that were built using construction techniques of the nineteenth century.

A garden is planted that is comprised of heritage plants typical of the era. Because of the authenticity of the buildings and grounds, the visitor will be able to see what an 1860s homestead would have looked like to the Gray and Reed families.

The homestead area is open year-round, and admission is free. People will find it a beautiful, serene place as they walk about. Because of the Civil War battle that happened here and the location of the Southwest Trail, this area is a landmark in our state's history.

Just like more famous battlefields, our historic battlefield has its own haunting, as we discussed earlier. This area is in a populated section of town, which can make is difficult to hear voices from the spirits. But if you happen to be there around dusk or dawn and you walk the perimeter of the battlefield, you just might hear what you're looking for: a disembodied voice.

This replica of a Civil War homestead was constructed using nineteenth-century construction techniques from fallen trees in the area. It is adjacent to the Reed's Bridge battlefield park. *Photo by David Hoge.*

It could be the spirit of a Native American who was forced to move from his motherland or a Union soldier who was just doing what he was ordered to do and suddenly became a spirit.

The following text is a portion of a poem written by Jim Barton of our state. I think he says it well.

The road runs south out of Jacksonville
'til it crosses this sluggish stream;
the fog hangs low on Bayou Meto,
and the past floats by like a dream.
Ghosts keep a watch on this crossing,
where Reed's Bridge used to stand,
And an army in blue was topped by a few
of the finest men in the land.

The park is open during the Halloween season, and the public is invited to visit the "Bloody Barn" and ride the "Haunted Hayride." The veil between life and death is very thin around Halloween time, causing some folks to believe that's why the spirits seem more active during that time.

CHAPTER 13

The Vanishing Point at Woodson Lateral

Woodson is a small community about fifteen miles from downtown Little Rock. Although the town started out as a railroad stop many years ago, today the trains pass through without any hesitation or stopping. The road leading directly west from Woodson, however, is the stuff of local legend. Some people believe they've seen a ghost on the road; others find it just plain spooky, night or day.

The quickest route to Woodson is on the road that bears its name, Woodson Lateral Road. It's accessed via Interstate 530, which begins at a junction with Interstates 30 and 440 and heads toward the southeast corner of the state. As you travel south on I-530 toward the Woodson exit—at mile marker 12—you might feel an adrenaline rush, especially if you are traveling at night. Will you see anything scary?

After you exit the freeway, you end up at a stop sign and will have arrived at your destination. Turn left and go back over I-530 heading east. Once you've crossed over the interstate, you get your first glimpse of the "road" before you.

Thick forest—some pine, some hardwood—grows on both sides and forms a canopy over the road. Unlike the cultured driveway at Augusta National or the tree-lined roads of France, the tunnel of trees on Woodson Lateral is too untamed, too overgrown to be completely pleasing to the eye. Trash lines the road, and broken trees and dead limbs on the side tell you that no one cultivates Woodson Lateral to be as good-looking as it could be. It feels desolate.

This exit sign from Interstate 530 indicates the turn off for Woodson Lateral Road. This area is known for its ghostly hitchhiker and other mysterious legends. The road alone is a chilling place and is frequented by local kids looking to get scared. *Photo by David Hoge.*

If you have a chance to notice the woods, you'll see that if you stopped and watched a person or animal walk directly into the woods, they would quickly disappear among the trees within twenty-five or fifty yards of you. But that is only during the daytime; at night, it's impossible to be certain of anything you see unless it's right in front of you.

Local high school kids like to dare each other to drive down the road at night and see if anything happens. One night, a couple decided to see if they could endure a dare. They started down the road about a mile into the "natural tunnel" and decided to stop. Darkness surrounded them, and they carried the dare further by turning off the engine. Total stillness and darkness surrounded them, and they felt as though they were in a black hole with no sense of direction.

Suddenly, a rustling of leaves was heard, and the young girl asked her friend to start the car and leave. Just as the lights were turned back on, a man appeared in front of the car and startled them so that their screams resonated through the woods. Needless to say, their adventure would be a tale told for the rest of their lives.

The road is fairly straight and level, although it has some dips that help create optical illusions. The roadway seems endless; its vanishing point also

Woodson Lateral Road, the location of a wreck that took the life of a young woman and her male companion nearly five decades ago, is a natural tunnel created by dense woods. People experience the illusion of a vanishing point as they travel this roadway. *Photo by David Hoge.*

plays tricks on the mind. Is that a vehicle coming? How long before it gets here? What is that I see down there by the side of the road? There's not much of a shoulder for making an emergency stop. Either side of the road has a steep drop-off. But the woods are so close to the road that a car skidding off Woodson Lateral won't go far before it gets hung up in the trees.

A fatal accident actually happened in which this scenario came true. A driver, who was reportedly speeding down the straightaway, flipped his car on its side. From that point, the car skidded off the road and careened into the woods, landing in between the trees. It was a very unusual accident, and emergency personnel had a difficult time extricating the driver from the car.

There are few houses along the way, and their driveways are secured by locked gates. There are even fewer security lights, so at night, pretty much only the headlights of your car and others illuminate the road and the tree tunnel. Driving at night can be dangerous because of the lack of light and the closeness of the woods to the road.

You see something far away, either on the road or next to it; is the bouncing of the light from oncoming headlights playing tricks on you? What if an animal dashes onto the road from the woods?

One rarely sees pedestrians on Woodson Lateral Road; the shoulder is too rough for walking and too narrow to allow you to walk comfortably away from traffic. So pedestrians stand out.

One such pedestrian may be the ghostly hitchhiker known to be around the area. Because of the terrain and limited shoulder access along the edge of the road, a woman who appears to be in distress would give cause for motorists to stop. She has been written and talked about for years and is thought to be the ghost of a woman who was in an automobile accident about fifty years ago.

The legend involves an accident on a rainy night and a couple who lose control of their car. The young man died in the accident, but the young woman survived long enough to seek help. She obviously suffered a traumatic death and is roaming while trying to figure out how to get home. Supposedly, the good Samaritan who picks her up and takes her to the house she talks about is surprised when she disappears at the house. Stories go that the house is vacant, or at other times, someone answers the door.

There are similar stories throughout our state, and it appears a ghostly hitchhiker is a common paranormal occurrence. Woodson Lateral Road's appearance is enough to scare someone, let alone an encounter with the ghostly hitchhiker.

Legends are interesting but cannot always be substantiated. However, the testimony from someone who has experienced such occurrences can seem believable. It just depends on whether the listener is willing to believe. I'm about to tell you of my experiences. I housesit in one of those houses along the road that is situated behind a locked gate. The description of the road and surrounding area comes from my personal experience.

I arrived at the house before the sun set so as not to have to drive down the road after dark. I did that only once and will not do it again. It was eleven o'clock at night and way too late and too dark for my liking. The headlights from my car shone brightly on the pavement, but due to the optical illusion, the road didn't appear to have an end. The experience made me feel as though I were falling.

On several occasions, between midnight and 2:00 a.m., the owner's dogs started barking. After checking things out, I found deer in the yard grazing. They seem to roam around this time of night. However, there have been times when the barking is caused by a light moving in the woods; is it human or paranormal? I don't know because I don't leave the security of the house to check it out, but I do continue to watch until whatever it is disappears. When I mentioned it to the homeowner, she told me about a light in another location, and all I could think of was, "Great, two unknown sources of moving lights."

The story of the ghostly lady hitchhiker will continue to excite those who hear it for the first time. They will be tempted to drive the road on a dark night to experience the adrenaline rush you receive in anticipation of your encounter. Her story will continue as a legend, but those of us who deal with the reality of what Woodson Lateral Road offers will just sit back and smile.

Perhaps new legends will entice high school students to continue their "frightful" night trips to the area and initiate their scare tactics by driving down the road with their lights off. As with most local lore and ghostly stories, only time will tell.

Woodson Lateral is a long road that covers several miles between two counties. Most of the road is peppered with homes, businesses and churches along the way, except for the three miles where these sightings have occurred. This stretch is the only place along the way that creates an eerie feeling as you begin your entrance. You see the other end of the road faintly in the distance and keep reminding yourself it's just the illusion of a vanishing point and you will eventually come to the end.

EPILOGUE

The words "spirit" and "ghost" make you think of an eerie feeling, misty images or shadowy figures. The emotional response to something that creates fear is a learned reaction. Along the way, probably in our young days as children, we became afraid of something and that feeling has stayed with us.

Let's give thought as to why apparitions occupy the places they do. For instance, a seemingly logical place would be a graveyard, where burials take place. Imagine a moonlit night and the effect the pale light would have on the granite tombstones and larger-than-life monuments. Shadows are cast as the moon travels across the sky, reflecting its light into the yard. I've seen this in Mount Holly Cemetery, and those eerie feelings surface quickly. It's also the same when there is no moonlight.

Perhaps a wooded area on a misty night makes one feel as though the mist flowing in the breeze is a gathering of ghosts. Certainly an old house with its gables and turrets sitting in an old part of town makes even the believer feel a little apprehensive. Why do these locations make us uneasy? Could it be simply our own life experiences?

Ghosts are around us everywhere. Old houses and buildings have just as many tales and legends as do modern-day structures. Actually, ghosts are a part of our everyday life; however, we may not recognize that. You have to be in tune with your surroundings and then you will realize that you're not alone.

For centuries, people all over the world have talked about ghostly visits, and their tales are described in the same way. A drop in temperature just

A view of Main Street in the early 1930s, looking north from the heart of downtown Little Rock. *Postcard courtesy of the Karcher Candy Company.*

before the ghost appears or a feeling that the room is full of people are common tales. Others tell of hearing disembodied voices and laughter or the sound of footsteps as though someone is walking nearby, yet no one is present.

Strange lights and distinctive odors such as perfume or tobacco are some of the unusual experiences shared by individuals. These events should lend truth to the fact that ghosts exist because many people of all ages from around the world have these unexplained experiences, and they are described the same way.

Recently, an article appeared in our local newspaper, the *Arkansas Democrat Gazette*, regarding the work of a psychiatrist named Dr. Elisabeth Kubler-Ross. She was a Swiss American doctor who researched near-death experiences and provided those studies to the world. While death and the process of dying are controversial subjects, her studies were informative and shed light on what happens.

Dr. Ross wrote *Death and Dying* in 1969, and it became an international bestseller. It explains the stages of dealing with death and the personal loss. What makes death a controversial subject? The fear of dying, the unknown of what we will experience during the process or the emotions felt knowing we are leaving something behind—our life and family—could all trigger this response.

It could be controversial because people don't like talking about dying and are uncomfortable with such discussions. The article said, "The book, based on years of her research findings and 20,000 cases of near-death experiences, concluded physical death is nothing to be feared."

"What the church tells little children about guardian angels is based on fact," Dr. Ross said, adding: "There is proof that every human being from birth to death is guided by a spirit entity whether you believe it or not."

Had it not been for the spirit of Mary Eliza Walters, I would not be writing this book. I had the opportunity to hear her voice on a recorder late one night, and I still experience the same chill each time I hear it. It's incomprehensible that a deceased person can speak, but as unbelievable as it is, it's true.

The first chapter of this book is about Curran Hall, Mary's home. If you have read the chapter, then you know she died before living in her beautiful house. Since her death, a century and a half ago, residents have told stories of her spirit's existence.

Curran Hall is not one of those scary-looking houses as someone might anticipate, but a warm, inviting place. It's the Little Rock Visitor Center, and more often than not, visitors comment on the comfortable feeling they have while in the house or garden. They feel at home. I think its Mary's spirit that people feel.

Whether one believes or accepts the paranormal is his or her personal choice, of course, but one should at least consider the possibility.

I hope that you have enjoyed reading about the haunted historic sites around Little Rock. Through investigations and historic information about these places, we've been able to find out who the spirits are, at least some of them. I accept that they exist and are trying to communicate with us; I hope that you will accept it, too.

Works Consulted

Websites

Arkansasties. www.arkansasties.com.

Baker House Bed and Breakfast. www.bedandbreakfast.com.

City of Little Rock. www.littlerock.org.

Empress Bed and Breakfast. www.theempress.com.

Encyclopedia of Arkansas History and Culture. www.encyclopediaofarkansas.net.

Jacksonville Museum of Military History. www.jaxmilitarymuseum.org.

MacArthur Museum of Arkansas Military History. http://arkmilitaryheritage.com/.

Mosaic Templars. http://www.mosaictemplarscenter.com/.

North Little Rock History Commission. www.nlrhistory.com.

Reeds Bridge. http://reedsbridgebattlefield.com/.

Wikipedia the Free Encyclopedia. http://en.wikipedia.org/wiki/Main_Page.

BOOKS

Christ, Mark K., and Cathryn H. Slater, eds. *Sentinels of History*. Fayetteville: University of Arkansas Press, 2000.

Cranford, Frances Anderson, Nancy Nixon McDonough and Mary Fletcher Worthen, eds. *Recipes in Perpetuity*. Printed in the United States of America: n.p., 2010.

Crawford, Sybil F. *Jubilee: The First 150 Years of Mount Holly Cemetery Little Rock, Arkansas*. Little Rock, Arkansas: August House, Inc., 1993.

Crawford, Sybil F., and Mary Fletcher Worthen, eds. *Mount Holly Cemetery Burial Index*. Little Rock, Arkansas: August House, Inc., 1993.

Mysteries of the Unknown—Phantom Encounters. Alexandria Virginia: Time-Life Books, 1988.

Roy, F. Hampton, Sr., Charles Witsell Jr. and Cheryl Griffith Nichols. *How We Lived: Little Rock As An American City*. Little Rock, Arkansas: August House, Inc., 1984.

About the Author

Linda Howell is a tour guide in Little Rock, Arkansas, who specializes in a variety of tours. She is the owner of Haunted Tours of Little Rock and provides the "Haunted Evening Tour," which encompasses many of the sites in this book. For centuries, members of her family have been interested in the paranormal and have had a strong belief in the afterlife and the possibilities that exist on the other side.

While working at the Little Rock Visitor Center, she discovered that the first and last owner of the house have been occupying it as spirits for years. There was enough evidence to warrant a paranormal investigation that resulted in capturing the spirits' voices on a digital recorder.

Although she doesn't consider herself to be a historian, Linda has an appreciation for history and a desire to learn as much as she can. This information has proved valuable on her tours.

With her knowledge of Little Rock's haunted places and a friendship with the paranormal community, she was inspired to develop the "Haunted Evening Tour." She enjoys sharing the history of the area with all tour groups, whether haunted or educational. One of the most frequent comments from visitors? "Little Rock is a well-kept secret."

For more information, visit www.hauntedtoursoflittlerock.com.